D0105064

Comforting One Another

In Life's Sorrows

Karen Mains

THOMAS NELSON PUBLISHERS
Nashville • Atlanta • London • Vancouver

Author's Note: Some names and situations have been disguised in order to protect the privacy of the individuals concerned.

Published in Nashville, Tennessee, by Thomas Nelson, Inc., Publishers, and distributed in Canada by Word Communications, Ltd., Richmond, British Columbia.

The poem "The Nuns of Vorkuta Prison" by Mark Rozema originally appeared in *Odd Angles of Heaven: Contemporary Poetry by People of Faith,* ed. David Craig and Janet McCann, (Wheaton, Ill.: Harold Shaw Publishers, 1994). The book has since gone out of print. All attempts were made to contact the poet for permission to reprint, but were unsuccessful.

Library of Congress Cataloging-in-Publication Data

Mains, Karen Burton.
Comforting one another : in times of sorrow / Karen Mains.
p. cm.
"A Janet Thoma book."
Includes bibliographical references.
ISBN 0-7852-7566-5 (hardcover)
1. Consolation. 2. Grief—Religious aspects—Christianity. 3. Mains, Karen Burton. I. Title.
BV4905.2.M275 1997
248.86—dc21 97-2280
CIP

Printed in the United States of America.

1 2 3 4 5 6 BVG 02 01 00 99 98 97

To
Douglas L. Mains,
father,
who has ever held us
and who holds us still.

CONTENTS

Part Four
The Final Pietàs

FOREWORD

Comforting One Another is not a list of principles to apply or prescriptions to take. What Karen Mains has dared to give us is her own intimate treatise on grace, what God has done for her personally during the last four years. This book is about fragments, brokenness . . . and glue. "Man is born broken. He lives by mending and the grace of God is the glue." We read her words and know we are not alone.

To write authentically is often times a rough and risky business. A writer balances the apple on his head as well as shots the arrow. "To know how to say what others only know how to think his head as well as shoots the arrow. "To know how to say what others only know how to think is what makes men poet of sage; and to dare to say what others only dare to think makes men martyrs or reformers—or both." (Elizabeth Charles, British writer, 1828-1896.)

I have known David and Karen Mains for more than twenty years. The journey of their life and ministry rings true. In 1993 Karen visited me and my family in Madrid. There, where I had hung up my metaphorical harp by the waters of Babylon, where my creative output had shriveled to less than a trickle, she brought Christ's presence to me in such a way that it brought health and accord to the abused, silenced fractions of my creative soul. Soon after she left I wrote a note of thanks to her husband. There is one line of affirmation and deep appreciation that I still recall: "For me, Karen's visit was the closest thing to an actual visit from Jesus that I have ever experienced."

Indeed, the universe is in exile. But as I have absorbed *Comforting One Another,* I have felt held. God's loving arms have reached out from between the lines and embraced me in a way that blots up my sorrows. I have been given the word *pietà* that I can use in offering to others this same holding in Jesus' name. My eyes have been opened to see within the common distress of humanity the embrace that saves.

My soul has been strengthened, and I have picked up my creative instruments again. If in my life I ever produce a "canvas" that offers calm to a catastrophic world, search my pockets when I die. The note of gratitude will be there.

Douglas Edward Kracht
Missionary Church Planter,
Artist in Exile

ACKNOWLEDGMENTS

In the making of a book, as in the making of a life, there are always many contributors. Both processes, writing and living, are dependent upon collaborators if we are to do either well. And I give grateful acknowledgment to those who have lent me strength for both.

First there are the holders, people who stand beside and freely give loyalty and steadfastness; my amazing children who have encircled me with the practical gifts of love and humor: Randall and Carmel, Doug and Melissa, Joel and Laurie, and Jeremy. Always there is David, my husband, who co-labors with me to establish this amazing dance we call marriage, but which touches deeper into mystery, a union certainly sacramental. Then there are the friends, my covenant community of prayer companions: Linda Adams, Adele Calhoun, Linda Richardson, Jane Rubietta, Marilyn Stewart, Sybil Towner; indeed we have often been a community of suffering friends; Gail MacDonald, who gives me an hour of phone time each month, and my walking partner, Scottie May.

Thanks to the early readers of a manuscript in process: Stephen Hayner, Sandy Wilson, Gail MacDonald again. To all those who gathered pietàs for me, many of which were not included in this book but that buoyed my soul as it struggled with the words on the page. To my editors: Janet Thoma, who tore the thing apart so I could put it back together again, a much better book the umpteenth time around, and Lila Empson, whose patience and kindness steadied me through the last weary stages of finishing everything as well as it was started. The words of Liz MacFazean, "Just tell yourself it will be beautiful," steadied my anxieties again and again and sent me into the task at hand with courage and determination to not be fainthearted.

To Dwight Ozard at *Prism Magazine* with whom I brainstormed the idea for the article "Holding the Broken Body," which became the basis for this book—even first concepts are conceived when another approves. Though *Comforting One Another* has become the name of this created child, it will always be called "Holding the Broken Body" to me. To Leighton Ford, who encouraged me more than he will ever know with his phone calls of kindness and interest in my fledgling journey into the tactile arts. To Richard Blackburn, art historian, who carefully corrected my critical analysis and whose educated attention assured me that I was "reading" the artworks with a sure inner instinct.

Indeed, all have been holders of one kind or another. And there are more, many more, but these are the ones who have mostly impacted my life and this writing. I am nothing, and how well I know it, without those who bear me their gifts; may I learn better how to bear gifts to them.

INTRODUCTION

The greatest fear I have in writing this very personal account is that people may find it self-serving. I am not interested in defending (or explaining) a book I wrote, *Lonely No More*, which became the subject of painful controversy. The reader is intelligent; he or she can find or borrow a copy and make a determination. Neither am I desirous of using the printed page to lambaste my enemies; generally, in a mud fight I'm the one who comes home with dirty hands.

My purpose in writing this book is to discover and work out on the pages what it is I have learned in the middle of an extremely painful season of my life. What were God's intents for me in the midst of this storm?

And our wilderness was real, not in any way manufactured. Because of the collapse of our donor base due to false accusations that we were not orthodox, David and I looked at the possibility of defaulting on the home equity loan we were forced to acquire in order to stabilize our payroll shortages.

Truly, it felt as though the demon of death was leering at us. One daughter-in-law, the wife of our eldest son, who served as the chief financial and operating officer of the ministry, became actively anorexic due to the daily stress of our collapsing environment. With two little ones to care for, she began a third pregnancy weighing only eighty-two pounds. The teenage child of an extended family member died tragically. We released 40 percent of our workforce. Those who remained coped with a series of death scenarios: the death of a parent, the suicide of a friend, the end of a marriage, the drowning of a grandchild.

In the fall of 1994, one donor and one lender provided $225,000 as a means to receive a matching grant from the New Era Foundation for Philanthropy; in May 1995, just before we were due to receive our first returns, the *Wall Street Journal* reported that the foundation organization had defaulted, losing some $53 million from not-for-profit institutions.

What were the lessons to be learned in all of this? For me the greatest lesson had to do with the meaning of mercy. I am learning to live within the mercy heart of God and to allow him to hold me within this shelter.

The situation has been seemingly unending and tough, but there have been hands waiting to help. The individual who loaned our ministry $100,000 for the New Era grant wrote it off as a charitable contribution. David's father, an ever-faithful contributor to the work of God, made working capital available as a low-interest loan. One overseas mission group (after checking with the Evangelical Council for Financial Accountability) gave us a donation and then floated another sizable loan. Our largest creditor bought our ministry buildings in a friendly sale as security against our debt. A publisher advanced the ministry money against print projects. A donor gave substantially out of his insurance settlement from a fiery car accident in which he was severely burned.

We have been held.

Neither do we have a happy ending to report; as of this writing things are still messy for the Mainses. There is no pat resolution to this story although there are improvements. We have miraculously reduced our debt by over a million, carried on ministry, mounted a national daily television broadcast, kept the family healthy and our key staff strong, and done the work with almost half the people needed. Creditors, for the most part, have been understanding.

Most important, I will never look at a desperate circumstance again without the awareness that God can make a way in the wilderness. Our role is to choose to trust and believe in his great and amazing capacities. I have discovered some awesome spiritual insights.

Consider these words: *Objects in the mirror are closer than they seem*. General Motors reminds me each time I check my side mirror that we live in a world where the unseen is very near.

The spiritual world, though not seen, is nevertheless close. The community of faithful witnesses surrounds us. We are embraced by the holy good, by the saints who have gone before us. Something greater than death is here, something larger than the life I know and understand.

We are being held.

Thank you, God.

Part One

On Holding

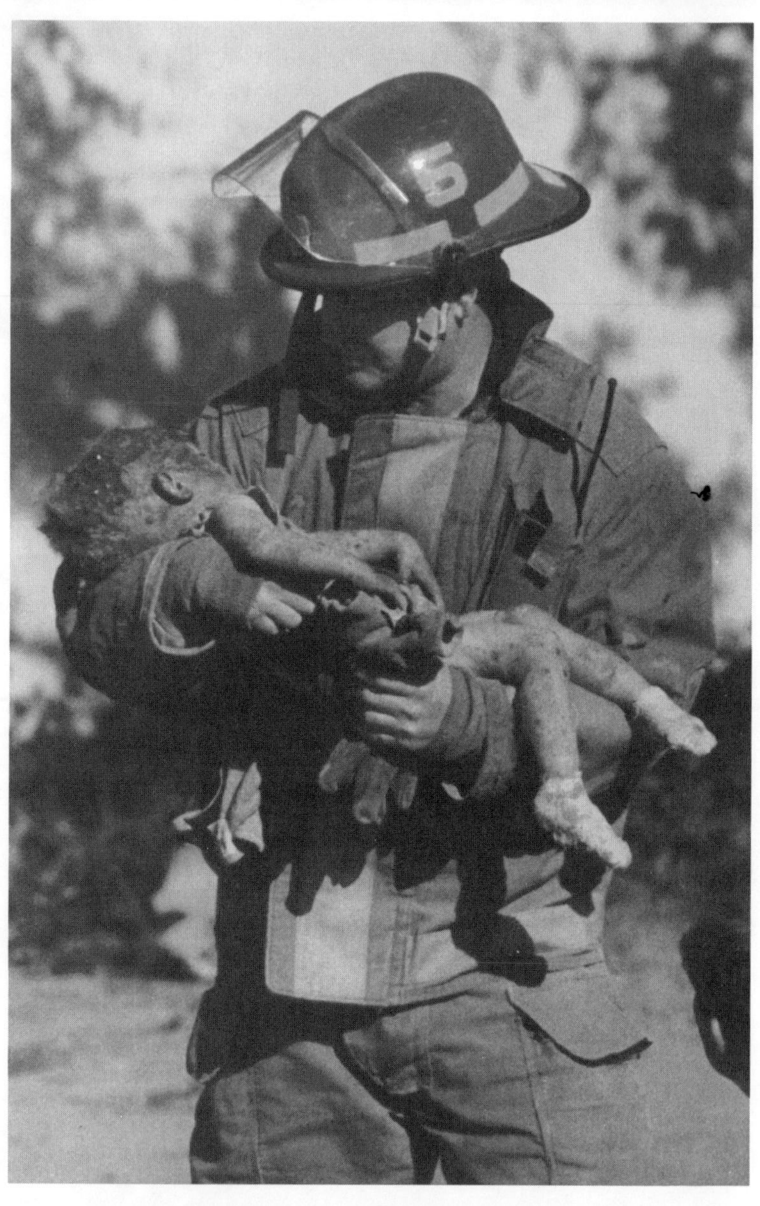

The images of the broken bodies of children being carefully carried out of the bombed-out ruins of the Alfred P. Murrah Building in Oklahoma City in 1995 touched us all. The "pietà" sentiment was explicitly portrayed as fire fighter Chris Fields carried the body of one-year-old Baylee Almon from the wreckage. *Photo by Charles H. Porter IV / SYGMA*

Chapter One

COLLECTING PIETÀS

The rescue worker, fireman Chris Fields, holds the broken body in his arms. Even in the news photograph, the deep gash shows, a cruel wound on the small round head. Is the child dead? Like the firefighter in this cover photo, we stare into the baby's face, hoping. Certainly, he has pulled her from the ruin in time, hasn't he? Surely there is a faint breath, some stirring of life. Yesterday, April 18, 1995, Baylee Almon turned one year old. This morning, a blast from an exploding Ryder rental van sent a blue-yellow fireball through the Alfred P. Murrah Federal Building, collapsing nine floors. The forty children in the America's Kids day-care center on the lower level were buried beneath tons of cement, flying debris, twisted girders, shattered glass.[1]

I looked at the *Newsweek* magazine cover again. Tearing out the page, I checked the inside photo credit: "Lester (Bob) LaRue;

Oklahoma Natural Gas." *A pietà*, I think. *A contemporary photojournalist pietà*.

During a season of my own sorrows I have been collecting pietàs. A pietà is any person or group of persons holding a body in death or a body near death. In its broadest sense a pietà is any time we give comfort to those trampled by life's sorrows. I find pietàs in film, in popular literature, in fine art, in real life. They blare the world's grief; like this one in *Newsweek*, they slap me in the face. And from each, I am learning how to hold the broken.

In shock the whole nation riveted its attention on the rescue efforts in Oklahoma City that fateful April morning. A kind of mass consciousness wondered, "What is this madness that detonates thousands of pounds of explosives on a workday morning in the heartland of America?"

"They've found a dead baby with yellow booties!" someone at the death site shouted. Aren Almon instantly knew it was her child.

The children became markers of the horror. A Red Cross worker, Jennifer Harrison, described their cries, "As we helped people on the street, we could hear children crying, like blowing in the wind. You couldn't see them. You just heard their voices."[2]

U.S. News & World Report writer Harrison Rainie protested this violation: "The most chilling fact about the bombing was that it struck at children eating breakfast."[3] Allowing himself anguish, he asked how this nation is to find words to grieve the children, then referred to the distraught Queen Constance, lamenting the loss of the prince in Shakespeare's *King John*. The queen's lament ends with words that voice the pathos of every grieving parent, "O, Lord! my boy, my Arthur, my fair son! / My life, my joy, my food, my all the world! / My widow-comfort, and my sorrow's cure!"[4] Wordless ourselves, literature is often the only way we can give eloquent voice to our distress.

A pietà. I am collecting pietàs.

And why? What causes them to catch my eye? Why are they so weighted with meaning for me?

The April 22 edition of the *Oklahoman & Times* reported:

> In the midst of the horror and chaos wreaked by the deadly bomb blast at the federal building in downtown Oklahoma City, ordinary citizens became heroes. . . . Acts of heroism, sacrifice, compassion, and dedication by countless people in the gut-wrenching, agonizing hours in the wake of the dastardly, murderous explosion were so numerous as to be almost commonplace."[5]

At the prayer service in Oklahoma City on April 23, 1995, four days after the blast, Dr. Billy Graham reminded a grieving community and a wary nation:

> Times like this will do one of two things. They will either make us hard and bitter and angry at God, or they will make us tender and open, and help us reach out in trust and faith. . . . A tragedy like this could have torn this city apart, but instead it united this city, and you have become a family. We have seen people coming together in a way we never could have imagined. . . . The forces of hate and violence must not be allowed to gain their victory—not just in our society, but in our hearts. Nor must we respond to hate with more hate. This is a time of coming together.[6]

The distresses of life are the circumstances that test our mettle. It is in suffering, large or small, that pain meets our human progress. In each of life's sorrows we are given a choice. In *Requiem for the Heartland,* a photojournalist's book that dedicates its proceeds to the victims of the bombing, one of the photos shows a woman reaching out to another, a stranger who was weeping. "I don't know who you are," she said, "but I know you need a hug."[7]

It is in these simple choices that we show a particular kind of private valor. One steps over or around or through the dividing walls of humanity. Why am I collecting pietàs? In the days left to me, I want to become a holder of the broken, someone who chooses to be a comforter for others facing life's sorrows. Pietàs teach me what this looks like. Pietàs give me pictures of the meaning of mercy in the midst of distress. From them, I am learning holding lessons.

In the play *Amadeus* by Peter Shaffer, the first act opens upon Salieri, once the court musician, who out of jealousy and envy had been the nemesis of the brilliant Wolfgang Amadeus Mozart, dead now for thirty-two years. Infirm, guilt-tormented, he is an inmate in a hospital for the mentally insane. *"Perdonami, Mozart! Il to assassino ti chiede perdono!"* the old man cries.[8] Pardon Mozart! Pardon your assassin! His attendants are shocked: Can this be true? Or are these the ramblings of a maddened mind? Salieri cries again, *"Pietà, Mozart! Mozart, pietà!"*

Mercy. Have mercy. At times in our lives we will cry for mercy. We will long for it from those we have wronged. We will plead for it at the hands of those who are misusing us. Our souls will harangue heaven. Pietà! Mercy. Have mercy.

"Mercy triumphs over judgment," writes James the Apostle.[9] And Scripture tells us that mercy and pity are important to God. The various Hebrew words that can be translated "mercy" are used over two hundred times in Scripture. Refrains like this one from Psalm 86 are intertwined through the pages again and again: "But You, O Lord, are a God full of compassion, and gracious, / Longsuffering and abundant in mercy and truth. / Oh, turn to me, and have mercy on me!"[10] Gerard Manley Hopkins, the great nineteenth-century poet, writes, "I say we are wound with mercy round and round—as with air."[11]

This is why I am collecting pietàs. I desire a soul expansive enough to grant this mercy to others in their moments of greatest need. Too often I am given to judgment. I do not want, like Salieri, to be guilty of complicity in the brokenness of others. Christ himself taught, "Be merciful, just as your Father also is merciful."[12]

So I am collecting. I am collecting pietàs.

What more recognizable image of the pietà than Michelangelo's flawless masterpiece. This sculpture, on display in the Vatican in Rome, brilliantly evokes the human in the divine and the divine in the human. *Photo courtesy of Corbis-Bettmann*

Chapter Two

Holding the Broken Body

Every Good Friday I attempt to remember the death of Christ while on my knees. A line in a poem by William Butler Yeats refers to a "slouching towards Bethlehem,"[1] but I think it is really Jerusalem toward which we slouch. Christ set his face toward this holy city; he trod intently toward the agony of redemption. I, on the other hand, want to avoid all pain, even that which will free me to live a righteous life. Most of the year I do a slipsliding two-step up holy hills, distracted, shuffling papers on the always crowded desks of my days.

But on Good Friday I attempt to remember the death of Christ on my knees. The Baptist Protestantism that has formed me often rushes into Easter. Yet churches that observe the calendar year of holy remembrances traditionally begin to "set their faces" toward Jerusalem with a Maundy Thursday liturgy. Somehow, I never seem to be able to make these services; the subway train of crammed living jostles aside my good intentions. So my yearly crucifixion vigil usually begins, not in the Upper Room, but in the Garden.

Watching in prayer is a hard-won discipline. Even as an adult my attention wanders; I become again a restless child. Mostly, I find myself empathetic with the lassitudes of the weary disciples. Most of them were, after all, rather young men.

The familiar Scriptures of that moment echo in my mind:

> Then Jesus came with them to a place called Gethsemane, and said to the disciples, "Sit here while I go and pray over there." And He took with Him Peter and the two sons of Zebedee, and He began to be sorrowful and deeply distressed. Then He said to them, "My soul is exceedingly sorrowful, even to death. Stay here and watch with Me."[2]

On Good Friday, 1993, around noon, I slipped into the chapel of the nearby Episcopal church where I often pray and was surprised at something I saw. Someone had positioned a low table before the altar. On it was set a linen cloth, a small crucifix, a pottery chalice filled with wine, and an earthenware plate holding Communion wafers.

A woman bustled in the nearby sacristy.

I called out to her: "What a wonderful aid to prayer!"

Often when my mind is wandering, it helps to have some token on which to fix my eyes. Postcards sent by friends—right now a copy of Monet's painting, *Morning with Willows*—are tucked in my desk organizer, a fixed point of beauty from which to build a center for concentration.

"Did you arrange this?" I asked.

Still finishing her tasks, she paused, calling back that the Communion elements were brought from the previous evening's Maundy Thursday service as a reminder to keep vigil over the broken body of Christ. Then, her work completed, she left me to the silence.

A few other watchers came that afternoon, but mostly I was alone. *What was it like,* I wondered, *to have kept vigil at the foot of the cross? What was it like for Mary?*

I have three sons, young men I love. How could I possibly bear to watch one of these sons die? How could I take one of them into my arms, crucified, flesh torn, form mauled? Would I hold the dead child to my bosom? Would shock benumb me? Could I lift my open palm in an eloquent gesture of acceptance? Or would I wail and rock and keen and mourn aloud the universal kaddish of all who have given life and then watched helplessly as death crawled close, clutched, then crumpled the beloved?

Would I shake my fist at God?

I thought back to the first time I became aware of Michelangelo's masterpiece the *Pietà*, which portrays Mary cradling the dead body of Christ on her lap. Michelangelo's five-century-old *Pietà* proved to be the 1964 World's Fair's single greatest attraction. On a busy day some hundred thousand people visited the Vatican Pavilion in Flushing Meadows, New York City, to view this drama of mother and son sculpted in Italy's finest marble.

The profound solemnity of this moment captures the ethos of a mother and son, now beyond torture, alone in the universe. Mary's head is bowed in prayer. Her left hand, palm up and open, appeals heavenward as though to say: *Do unto me according to your will*. A gesture of acquiescence.

Some art historians suggest that Mary might be a projected idealism of Michelangelo's mother, who died when he was just six years old. Flawless in its classicism, exquisitely finished, the sculpture brilliantly evokes the human in the divine and the divine in the human. Seven years after Columbus discovered America, Michelangelo, at age twenty-four, completed this masterwork. Recognized to be a consummation of fifteenth-century art, it established the artist's reputation in his own time.

In 1964, the 6,700-pound sculpture was taken from its dimly shadowed chapel at St. Peter's in Rome, attached to a vibration-proof base, crated, then submerged in tiny plastic dylite beads for the ocean voyage to the United States. It was addressed from Pope Paul VI of Rome to Cardinal Francis Spellman of New York. The packing case was lashed to the deck of the *Cristofor Colombo* with bindings that would release if the ship sank. Floating, a blinker would then mark its position, and a radio would send a distress SOS for rescue. The Vatican insured the *Pietà* for $25 million against damage during its nineteen-month stay at the World's Fair.[3]

During that same year, my husband, David, and I moved to nearby Chicago, where he had accepted a job as associate pastor at historic Moody Memorial Church. For me, this displacement from suburbia was the beginning of a long journey into discovering how much of my Christianity was an osmosis of inherited religiosity. I would soon be horrified to find racism hidden in my heart, would be challenged by the dialogue of the counterculture movement of the sixties and seventies, and would begin to come to terms with my own pro forma faith.

At the time of the 1964 World's Fair, I was learning a little about the economics of poverty, a little about the dialectics of politics, a little about the relationship of the gospel to the social ills that surrounded me, and a little about the New Testament call to community. But I knew nothing about pietàs. I had never really stared suffering in the eye.

We started a church on the impoverished West Side of Chicago in 1967 with a faithful handful of co-laborers. We were all filled with utopian evangelicalism, intent upon making the church what we felt a church should really be. At twenty-two years of age, I had already birthed two of our four children. Though dismayed about the failures of Christianity, I was filled with idealism and eagerness. Brokenness—my own or that of the world around me—did not as yet bear a recognizable face.

If we have eyes to see, however, we will find brokenness in the labor of artists. Michelangelo's *Pietà*, or any grieving mother, is a typology of tragedy, replicated throughout the centuries. Woman is not only the giver of life, she is often the one who keeps lonely vigil at life's end. Consider these contemporary pietàs: an African-American mother grieving her child, gang slain. an impoverished refugee bearing a starving child to her sunken breast. A woman, graveside, her eyes stark, hugging in her arms the militarily folded flag taken from her son's coffin. An ancient Marian prayer captures it all: "You have often slept on my lap the sleep of infancy, now you sleep on my lap the sleep of death."[4] Ultimately, sooner or later, in some way, man or woman, we all come face-to-face with death. This is the universal inevitability.

Those who study word origins, or etymology, find that in Italian, *pietà* originally referred to "dutiful conduct." Dante, elevating the simple and beautiful Florentine Italian over the more formal Latin, equated the word *pietà* in the *Inferno* and *Convivo* with the sentiments of pity, mercy, compassion, and lament.[5]

Giorgio Vasari, a contemporary of Michelangelo and one of his students, used *pietà* in his classic work *The Lives of the Artists* to refer to Christ himself as the pietà, rather than the form of mother and son. He wrote about "a painting of Pietà on the lap of our lady."[6] Some art historians, tracing precedents, label these types of studies as "lap-type lamentations" or "lamentations on the lap of. . . ."[7] Over the centuries, the artistic term *pietà* has evolved to mean any grouping in which someone holds or keeps vigil over a body in death, or over a body near death.

After a while on that Good Friday in 1993, all my prayer companions slipped away. *If I leave*, I thought, *who will keep vigil over this broken body of Christ? Could I not watch one more hour*? I had no festival meal to prepare. My husband was traveling, away from home in ministry. The children had their own plans. There was no urgent work demanding my attention.

Yes, I decided. I could watch. I could pray until someone else came to take my place. I recalled the Scripture of that first Good Friday:

> He went a little farther and fell on His face, and prayed, saying, "O My Father, if it is possible, let this cup pass from Me; nevertheless, not as I will, but as You will." Then He came to the disciples and found them sleeping, and said to Peter, "What? Could you not watch with Me one hour?"[8]

I began to think of all the people I knew whose souls were close to Golgotha. Friends— one whose wife was dying from cancer, another whose mother was terminally ill.

Who was it I held in my arms? My husband, certainly, weary with too much work and too little funding. Each night as he came to bed, I made it a practice to hold him and pray for his weary body, to ask that his rest would be deep and his dreams ones that restore well-being.

I also held in my arms the new generation, my infant grandchildren, for whom I felt more terror than I ever felt for my own children, knowing now how hazardous life really is.

Who was it I held in my praying arms? My colleagues in parachurch ministries over whose souls I watched as they served the Lord and journeyed into the death of self.

Kneeling in that little chapel, I began to recognize the living pietàs in my own life.

A Season of Sorrows

Like many, I am a person with a modicum of artistry. My gifts, in comparison to those few great Ulysseses of letters, are small. In addition, these abilities have had to survive the vicissitudes of motherhood and wifehood and homemaking. A lifetime of ministry has crowded me with additional responsibilities, and volunteerism in church and parachurch life have demanded my attentions. The artistry appointed to me is not large enough to drive me mad if I do not express it—just medium enough to make me neurotic. And even for small artists, the principle remains: That which is not used is lost. So I write.

However, it had become clear to me over the last decade that my small artist's breath was being strangled by some sort of ecclesiastical umbilical cord. The innumerable filters of doctrinal appropriateness that exist in my conservative branch of Christendom were choking the little artistry that did exist. Something of art in my soul was laboring to be birthed, and I was not midwife enough to give it life.

So I decided that my next book would be an exercise in telling the truth. Would I show forth the work of the Holy Spirit within me? Could I do it without jargon and didactic crutches? Could I successfully contemporize the classic devotional language and experience?

My editor and I wrestled mightily to break the style formulas that were choking my growth. I threw away two complete treatments, begged extended deadlines, and labored for three years, writing almost constantly, to finish a rather small book, and one quite different in its postpartum life from the original text. Even delayed, the birth was still premature, induced too soon by production schedules. Another four or five months would have given me time to rest from this overlong gestation, look the baby in the face, and say, "Oh, this is what you are called!" I knew *Lonely No More* was not a perfect child.

Once the book was published in 1993 critics labeled me apostate, heretical. I was accused of occult practices, of shamanism, of being counterfeit, of leading the flock astray through my writings. Newsletters decrying the book circulated, imposing meanings that I had never intended nor experienced. My name was mentioned detrimentally in the religious media. Even earlier books of mine, which had received awards from evangelical publishing associations, were back-scanned and sections quoted out of context as evidence of my error. Only one of my critics contacted me before writing negatively about me. None of them thought it important to forewarn me. None of them invited me to respond to their criticisms. Most chilling of all, I truly believe that none of them intended me personal harm.

My husband's national radio ministry was put into jeopardy. Station managers began to cancel *The Chapel of the Air,* which had been in existence for more than fifty years, broadcasting six days a week over some five hundred outlets. Though we had paid hundreds of thousands of dollars in airtime fees, contracts were broken without negotiation. Meeting planners began canceling my speaking schedules. Pastors called inquiring as to my orthodoxy. My husband was accused of being New Age.

This campaign was to continue for fifteen months. I requested that my publisher declare the book out of print and let it sell out in stores.

Donor revenues for *The Chapel of the Air* faltered at a time when our economic margins (always sparse) were extremely thin, due to our launching new ministry ventures to help the local church. Our staff was distracted from their work by having to conduct crisis management. Our most significant ministry tool, "The Fifty Day Adventure," a yearly spiritual growth program for families, small groups, and local parishes, dropped from a projected participation of 750,000 to 350,000, severely crippling our income and pushing us into debt.

I descended deeply, deeply into pain, which extended into seasons of suffering—spring, and then summer, fall, winter, and spring again. I do not mind—much—being corrected in my creative output; that is the nature of public life. But to be labeled evil, to be the object of gossip and slander—this strikes at the core of who I think I am before God and at my desire to serve him with a pure heart. In addition, I have always hated notoriety, to be featured in columns and magazine articles. We had to preempt our regularly scheduled broadcast through satellite feed and go nationwide for two weeks, explaining the nature of the criticisms against us and our response.

During this period of suffering I knew I had to live existentially in the Scriptures if I was going to emerge unharmed. This medicinal preserves us all. The Scriptures comfort us with the knowledge that others have been there before and have survived with their integrity intact. The prophet Jeremiah lamented:

> My enemies without cause
> Hunted me down like a bird.
> They silenced my life in the pit
> And threw stones at me.
> The waters flowed over my head;
> I said, "I am cut off!"
> I called on Your name, O LORD,
> From the lowest pit.
> You have heard my voice:
> "Do not hide Your ear
> From my sighing, from my cry for help."
> You drew near on the day I called on You,
> And said, "Do not fear!"[9]

Painful seasons force us to look carefully into our own hearts. A page in my prayer journal of 1993 is headed "Confessions of a Critical Woman":

> I have had judgment in my heart toward those in Your body. Forgive me for my past errors. Heal the inward darkness that exists within me. Give me, instead, such an embraceable love for Your people that my heart can scarce contain it. Help me to

guard myself from further errors in condemnation. I pray this, Lord, my God.

During seasons of suffering, we had better consider the Crucifixion. If in error, as my critics accused, I needed to look to the Cross. If not in error, even more the need to gaze long at Calvary. At the foot of the cross, one thinks much about the meaning of being reviled, of being betrayed, of being wounded for transgressions, of being spit upon and excoriated, of being counted as a vile offender. It is here, at the cross, that we learn to die.

George Mueller, the Englishman renowned for his work with orphans, once told someone who questioned how he could sustain such devoted service:

> There was a day when I died. Died utterly; died to George Mueller, his opinions, preferences, tastes, and will—died to the world, its approval or censure—died to the approval or blame even of my brethren or friends—and since then I have studied only to show myself approved unto God.[10]

Standing at the foot of the cross puts all suffering into proportion. Amy Carmichael, the missionary to India who spent much of her life rescuing girls given to temple prostitution, once wrote, "There are times when nothing holds the heart but a long, long look at Calvary. How very small anything that we are allowed to endure seems beside that Cross."[11]

Here, in this place of blood, we watch Christ die, and hopefully, in the watching, we learn slowly to lift our hands, like Michelangelo's Mary, with an open palm and gesture, "Give me joy, please, in all the workings of your will. I accept. I surrender. Teach me how to acquiesce to my own demise."

If I believe in a God who is sovereign, I must believe that he has a plan, perfect in his workings, to create exactly what he wants to create in me through my difficulties.

I do not like this bitter path before me. Compliance to my own suffering galls me, but I know it is important for me to bow my head before this pain. I must not strategize a campaign to restore my reputation. I must not get into dialogue with my accusers. There is a work of God going on in me, and I must not use up the energies I need to hold myself constant to an attitude of surrender. I must use this little season of pain to learn how to identify with Christ's suffering. Yet admittedly, I slouch toward Jerusalem, I sleep in Gethsemane, I stand silent at Golgotha.

And I am collecting pietàs.

Why have I been collecting pietàs? Because I need to learn better how to hold broken bodies: how to hold Christ's body broken in the world, how to hold his shattered church and the people who are the church. We are a people made to love and to receive love, to know and to be known, to hear and to be heard, to celebrate the beauty in humanity and to celebrate our own beauty as individuals. And our own brokenness always keeps us from these embraces that heal. We do not know how to hold and we do not know how to allow ourselves to be held.

The symbol of the cross, once a signifier of torture and of the painful cost of devotion, has now become a fashion statement, trivialized on every jewelry counter, bouncing between the breasts of performers who live their lives in every way but the way of the one who gave himself on the cross. When the symbols that interpret the deepest meanings of our faith become commonplace or misused, they lose their ability to point us to truth. What was startling becomes mundane.

The holy becomes desacralized by those with profane understandings as well as by us, followers of Christianity, who make the sacred hackneyed and who forget that in the most ordinary the holy often hides. Neither of these groups, consequently, can be shaken much by truth. (For truth is always shocking, jolting us at the foundations of comfortableness and familiarity. That is why we hate it so.) We must be, need to be, startled. New symbols rudely interrupt our pat routines with their clamor; they bump our souls, grown stodgy and lumpish, into some stumbling momentum.

That is why I am collecting pietàs. I do not know well how to hold the broken body; I am selfish and afraid, inattentive, unconnected.

Time has passed since that Good Friday of 1993 when I kept a lonely watch over Christ's body, symbolized by the bread and wine. The meditation begun that day extended into years of loss and heightened pain. Now I know for certain that those who commit themselves to keeping vigil over the broken body will in all likelihood become broken as well. I will still say yes. I will pray with more worthy fathers and mothers who have gone before me, *Teach me well the way of the cross*. I cannot hold to my breast the broken body of Christ in his church and in this world if I am not willing to become broken too.

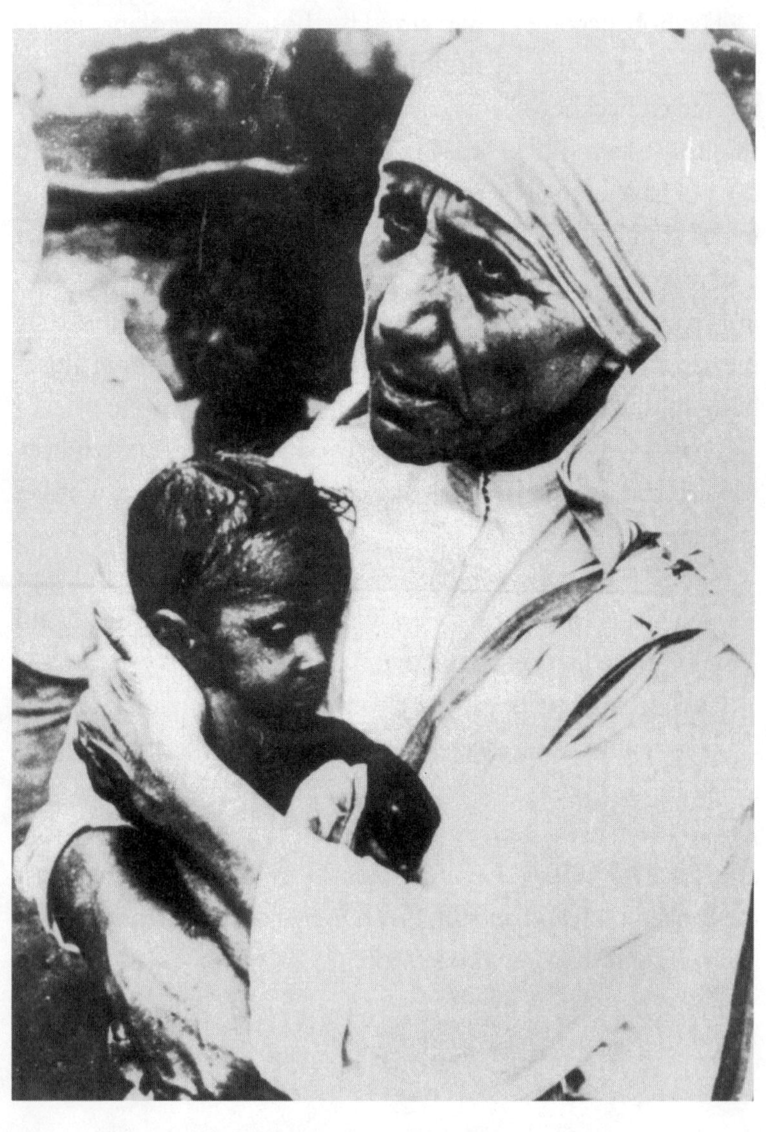

Mother Teresa and the other Sisters of Charity seek out the sick, the broken, and the dying to offer them the comfort they desire in a world that has rejected them. *Photo by UPI/Corbis-Bettmann*

Chapter Three

The Mercy Bearers: Those Who Hold

The windows of the lounge in the Mill Race Inn overlooked an ice-clogged Fox River, which meandered slowly through Geneva, Illinois. Outside, in the waning afternoon light, a gaggle of geese waddled in their winter fat around the frozen edge of a pond. Inside, Amy Harwell and her friend Polly Aschom attempted to describe to me the "hospice hold," a technique Fox Valley Hospice workers are trained to use with those who are dying. Though listening intently, I still couldn't quite imagine what this therapeutic embrace looked like.

"You mean that the hospice worker crawls right up on the bed beside the patient?"

Yes, was the answer, though both women were careful to make clear that this particular hold was to be utilized only when trust had been established, only at the patient's request, and only if the worker felt comfortable giving it.

Amy, an international speaker and business consultant, has written two books—*When Your Friend Gets Cancer* and *Ready to Live, Prepared to Die*—both of which evolved from a 1985 diagnosis of rapidly progressing cancer (invasive cervical cancer with bilateral lymph node involvement and metastasis to one lung). Polly, an elegant middle-aged woman and a hospice-trained friend, had become her mainstay.

Because the experimental treatment of chemotherapy, radiation, and surgery for Amy's cancer was successful (the odds for survival five years after diagnosis are fewer than twenty women in a hundred), she brought pertinent back-from-the-brink-of-death insights to bear on our dialogue. She has also used her considerable organizational skills to form a nonprofit ministry, *Joshua's Tent,* to help prepare others to die and to assist their loved ones faced with such a prospect.

That December afternoon, after the luncheon crowd had departed and before the after-work "happy hour" clientele arrived, we sat in the lounge in the winter light, sipping tea. We talked intently about the importance of a human presence during those moments when life seems to be ebbing away—literally or figuratively, emotionally or physically.

Words, however, proved inadequate.

"Oh, let's just show you," said Amy. A quick scan of the room, then both of them slipped to the floor. (Fortunately, we were tucked in a far corner and the lounge was almost empty.)

The women sat facing one another, Amy's legs stretched out as though in bed, and Polly's legs in the opposite direction (toward an imaginary headboard). Amy started to slide completely downward when she had a thought, lifted her head, and reminded me, "Try and picture the fact that I was hooked up to all kinds of tubes and contrivances: a nasogastric tube, a portable catheter, a uterine catheter, a basic intravenous line, and some others I probably can't remember. This hold enables the hospice worker to get close to the dying patient, despite obstructing hospital technology." Then down flat she went.

The two women, facing opposite directions, scooched together somewhere at the hips, as though crowding on a narrow bed. Polly, sitting upright, twisted her torso and leaned to her right. Then she cradled her left arm behind Amy's back, pulling her up from the floor, and extended her right arm under Amy's left shoulder. At the same time she slipped her slightly bent knees behind Amy's back to support her spine. In turn, Amy tucked her right arm around Polly's back and her left arm around Polly's neck. Polly rolled slightly backward pulling Amy's body forward, then she gently embraced her in this rocking motion—back and forth, back and forth, back and forth. I understood why some termed this technique the "hospice cradle rock." It was the kind of embrace one would use with an infant or hurting child.

Here was another pietà: a living pietà.

"What did this do for you, Amy, when you were sick?" I asked.

The two women still sat on the floor, intimately intertwined, and looked up at me.

"I cried," she answered with a smile. "That was the first time in the whole journey through cancer, from diagnosis to chemotherapy and surgery, that I had been able to release all my repressed emotions. I felt as though I was safe enough to let my ego collapse and just be a child. Someone who knew what she was doing would keep me from coming apart."

It is one thing to watch two apparently healthy women sit on the carpeted floor of a popular restaurant in a well-heeled suburban community, but it is quite another to witness this embrace enacted in a moment of life-and-death despair.

Driving home from the afternoon tea in Geneva, I tried to picture more clearly the now lively and vibrant Amy Harwell as a dying patient, and Polly, the dignified hospice worker, crawling right onto the bed of death and disease, tubes looping and cascading. I imagined silence; I imagined the soft glow of the overhead neon bed lamp. Against that, I imposed this modern-day pietà. Two women rocking—back and forth, back and forth. One weeping.

This pietà is a picture of tender mercy, I thought. And for the first time I began to understand that all pietàs are physical representations of mercy. One of the reasons I was so drawn to them, I suspect, was that during my own small season of sorrows I knew what it meant to need mercy. Intuitively, my artistic instincts had begun to gather these renderings in literature, art, and film so I could think deeply about the meaning of each.

Mercy. Holders, those who embrace another passing through or descending into death, are those rare humans so filled with this quality of godlike, tender compassion they are impelled to action.

I, too, want to be a doer of mercy, someone compelled to tender deeds.

At my request, the Fox Valley Hospice organization sent me several brochures describing their services. All hospice groups differ from region to region I am told, depending on the kind of funding that underwrites them and upon the people who administrate their services. This particular organization was community-based, nonprofit, and nondenominational; its outreach coordinates teams of caregivers to assist all who request help because of a life-threatening illness. The program involves the patient's primary physician, along with a hospice care coordinator, hospital chaplain, and trained volunteers, all of whom form the circle of protection that supports (or holds) the patient and his or her family.

When I phoned later with inquiries, the director explained, "We try to emphasize the importance of giving emotional and psychological support as well as physical care. . . . The cradle hold is designed to give comfort to those whose life is slipping away. We teach our hospice workers to connect with as much body surface as possible. When life is shattered, it feels as though there is no framework. For the dying to be embraced seems, literally, as though someone is holding them together."

Interestingly, there is a precedent for the hospice hold in the Bible:

> Now King David was old, advanced in years; and they put covers on him, but he could not get warm. Therefore his servants said to him, "Let a young woman, a virgin, be sought for our lord the king, and let her stand before the king, and let her care for him; and let her lie in your bosom, that our lord the king may be warm." So they sought for a lovely young woman throughout all the territory of Israel, and found Abishag the Shunammite, and brought her to the king. The young woman was very lovely; and she cared for the king, and served him; but the king did not know her.[1]

The oddity of this passage has always puzzled me, but since collecting pietàs, I now view it more sympathetically. Undoubtedly, there are dark moments so desperate that we need someone to come along side us: to get up into the deathbed, as it were, if only figuratively; to hold us tightly, to rock us gently, to protect and cover us so that we feel safe enough to let the grief and anguish rise. These strong ones hold us, often silently, so we will not be blasted apart by the terror that is shattering our identities. These wise ones understand that they hold us not to keep us (to possess or control us), but to give us strength. But they do more than just hold us; many, knowing mercy in its sublimest sense, lift us up to God, lift our pain and sorrow, our emotion-shredding dismay, in ways we are incapable of doing for ourselves.

Of course, holding is not limited to care for the dying. The living also need to be held. Prominent neurologist Oliver Sacks has learned the benefit of holding from a high-functioning autistic person, Temple Grandin, and her innovative "squeeze machine."

The Squeeze Machine, A Unique Comfort

Dr. Sacks describes the squeeze machine in his book *An Anthropologist on Mars* in a chapter that closely examines the life of Temple Grandin. With a Ph.D. in animal sciences, Grandin is an expert in the design of technological systems for animal management—farms, feedlots, corrals, slaughterhouses. Despite her accomplishments, she describes the difficulties of her autistic condition as leaving her often to "feel like an anthropologist on Mars."[2]

Autistic individuals, though greatly differing one from another and while suffering from a complexity of causes and effects, share a core and consistent triad of impairments: the impairment of social interaction with others, the impairment of verbal and non-verbal communication, and the impairment of play and imaginative activities. As Temple explained about herself to Dr. Sacks, "the emotion circuit's not hooked up—that's what's wrong."[3]

Grandin's intellectual capacities and adapting abilities enable her to understand the paradoxes of her own existence as a high-functioning autistic. Her autobiography, *Emergence: Labeled Autistic,* revisits the world of her childhood, a place where sensations were heightened, sometimes beyond endurance. It was a condition Sacks describes as "this almost unintelligible childhood, with its chaos, its fixations, its inaccessibility—this fierce and desperate state," which had almost led to her institutionalization at the age of three.[4]

At age five, longing to be physically held, she was nevertheless overwhelmed with the typical autistic terror of being embraced by humans. She began to create the concept of a magic machine that could squeeze her but over which she could also maintain control.

Growing up in farming and ranching communities, she became fascinated with the squeeze chutes that were designed to hold and restrain calves. A sympathetic high-school science teacher took her fixation seriously, challenging her to create her own "holding machine," one that would satisfy the need for the safety of deep holding without the attending paralyzing anxiety. The experience and encouragement led eventually to her pursuing a professional career in animal sciences. Both before and after writing her doctoral thesis, she conducted intensive research on the influence of deep pressure on autistics, as well as on college students and even animals. Today her "holding machine" is undergoing clinical testing. She has become a foremost designer of squeeze chutes for cattle management and is a leading proponent on the theory and practice of humane restraint.

Temple Grandin's personal holding machine, which is kept in her bedroom, is essentially a two-sided box, joined to a backboard in the shape of a V. Upholstered, with a control panel to one side, it is powered by an industrial compressor similar to the kind used to inflate car tires. Demonstrating the "squeeze machine" for Oliver Sacks, Temple crawled facedown into the V and stretched out to her full length. After starting the compressor and turning the controls, the sides of the box pressed inward, holding her firmly.

Once she was in the machine, Sacks noticed that Grandin seemed more relaxed and that her voice softened. She testified herself that being in the box was one of the few times when she could feel love, both for and from other people. In the safety of the holding machine, she became relaxed enough to experience empathy for others, a state not readily available to her because of the "disconnection of the emotional circuit."[5]

None of the pietàs I have collected are more fascinating than Temple Grandin's holding machine. It speaks to me of many things—of the need we humans have to be held even in the face of our wild and varied disorders. Of the fact that the need to be held is so basic a human drive that we will go to any adaptive measures (positive or negative) to create a holding experience. It teaches me that there are many holding lessons to be learned, even from the squeeze machine created by an autistic savant. But mostly it informs me that when holding conditions are healthy, when they provide protection and safety, people can, despite enormous limitations, develop empathy for others.

For the Christian, holding becomes a sacramental act. The holder does much more than he or she knows; the one being held receives more than he or she can understand. And of course the holder may hold in ways other than just the physical.

I personally have been held by those stalwart warriors who never touched me, but I was lifted up by their presence until I was convinced again that Christ, indeed, was near. This concrete steadying occurs on such profound levels, it is as though God himself is embracing us.

Holding can be as slight as the touch of a hand, and it can come from a stranger, from someone we don't even know.

THE TOUCH OF A HAND

I noticed the stylish African-American woman, elegantly wrapped in a mink coat, in the hotel lobby as we both waited for a van to take us to the St. Louis airport. Politely, we nodded to one another while boarding, but neither of us exchanged words.

I was weary from ministering at a weekend retreat, but mostly, as in lonely moments like this, I became absorbed with painful thoughts of the criticisms and accusations leveled at *The Chapel of the Air Ministries*. The year had been unsettling to us all, but the effect on me was often vicious, bending me, to my great frustration, emotionally low.

"My dear sister," said the woman beside me as the shuttle driver parked the van curbside, yelled "United," and jumped out to get my luggage.

She reached over and gently touched my arm. "My dear sister," she said, "you are in such pain and distress, I am going to pray for you. I am going to pray for you all the way home on my flight." She held my arm, reaching across racial barriers, reaching across possible impropriety.

"Oh, thank you," I responded, wanting ever so much to throw myself into her furry embrace, just to be held. "Pray that I will be protected from the evil one."

I dismounted the van, collected my baggage, and never saw the woman again. But for months, her words, her love, her concern warmed me each time I knelt to pray. I could feel the touch of her hand.

I still can.

This stranger gave me mercy.

The Blessing of Mercy

The psalmists well knew the need for comfort and mercy. Psalm 71 is the journal of an aging saint:

> Deliver me, O my God, out of the hand of the wicked (v. 4).
>
> By You I have been upheld from birth (v. 6).
>
> Let them be covered with reproach and dishonor
> Who seek my hurt (v. 13).
>
> Now also when I am old and gray-headed
> O God, do not forsake me (v. 18).
>
> You, who have shown me great and severe troubles,
> Shall revive me again,
> And bring me up again from the depths of the earth.
> You shall increase my greatness,
> And comfort me on every side (vv. 20–21).

The Hebrew Old Testament words that deal with mercy are basically three: *hesed, hanan,* and *raham*. All these can be rendered as "loving-kindness," "goodness," and "heartfelt compassion." Throw into this mix a Greek word from the New Testament, *charis*, which means "grace," and you have the wide parameter that encompasses the divine concept of mercy.[6] These words appear hundreds of times in the Old and New Testaments. Most describe God's character, such as this song of praise:

> Bless the LORD, O my soul;
> And all that is within me, bless His holy name!
> Bless the LORD, O my soul,
> And forget not all His benefits:
> Who forgives all your iniquities,
> Who heals all your diseases,
> Who redeems your life from destruction,
> Who crowns you with lovingkindness and tender mercies,
> Who satisfies your mouth with good things,
> So that your youth is renewed like the eagle's.[7]

We need to mirror God's mercy to the world through actions and images, as well as our words.

Often I am amazed at how close the art forms of our culture come to mirroring the meaning of our spiritual realities. I noted this in 1973 when Eugene O'Neill's *A Moon for the Misbegotten* was revived on Broadway by director Jose Quintero. Intensely autobiographical, this was the last play O'Neill wrote before his death. The original 1947 production was a disaster from start to finish. Running into adverse criticism on the road and hounded by censors, the play closed. When the New York Theater Guild, two years later, attempted to recast and remount it, the playwright protested, "I don't believe I could live through production." And O'Neill did not live to see it performed again.[8]

Through the kindness of friends, David and I sat with the theater audience for Quintero's revival. Colleen Dewhurst played the giant of a woman, Josie Hogan, and Jason Robards balanced her strength with his own portrayal of the tortured, alcoholic Jim Tyrone. Critical raves not only resurrected O'Neill's posthumous reputation, but escalated the careers of Dewhurst, Robards, and Quintero.

The play deals with two misbegottens whose lives intersect in a small town in Connecticut. Josie is a woman so ungainly and powerful no man can contend with her. She encourages a fictional reputation that she is the region's loose woman. Jim carries the weight of his own failures and betrayals and is sinking into a living death, an alcoholic stupor. But grace is unrestrainable, even in the writings of O'Neill. The two characters sense the true beauty in each other's souls, hidden deep beneath the desperate charades, the multiplying lies of their everyday lives.

In the third act, beneath the moon, an epiphanic juncture occurs. Each reveals the truth about the other. Josie is really a virgin capable of sacrificial love, says Jim. And he, says Josie, is really a man longing for forgiveness and redemption. Sitting together throughout the night, on the rickety porch steps of the old farmhouse, Josie takes the tortured man into her arms. He has been yearning to rest his weary head on her breast.

Center stage, on Broadway, the pietà forms, a contemporary lap-type lamentation. She knows he is facing death—death of soul, death of spirit, death of body.

Josie. Forgive my selfishness, thinking only of myself. Sure, if there's one thing I owe you tonight, after all my lying and scheming, it's to give you the love you need, and it'll be my pride and joy. It's easy enough, too, for I have all kinds of love for you—and maybe this is the greatest of all—because it costs so much. Jim! Don't look like that!

Jim. Like what?

Josie. It's the moonlight. It makes you look pale, and with your eyes closed—

Jim. You mean I look dead?[9]

Jim Tyrone falls asleep with Josie holding him through the third act and into the fourth, when he finally wakes and exits. The play ends with Josie's benediction: "May you have your wish and die in your sleep soon, Jim darling. May you rest forever in forgiveness and peace."[10]

And the New York audience, illiterate for the most part on theologies about the redemption and sacrament, nevertheless leaned close, straining toward the stage in what I could only conclude was the powerful desire all people have to be held at the moments of deepest need. Even in theatrical experience, humans are drawn by portrayals of lap-type lamentations. The intellect may reject this need, but the soul comprehends and reads pietàs in its own language. As Pascal in the *Pensées* once explained, "The heart has reasons that reason does not know."[11]

Those of us who say we follow Christ, the mercy-giver, must learn to frame similar pietàs in our own creative works. This is extremely important if we are to convey our most cherished belief in the mystery of God incarnate in human flesh, a difficult truth for even devoted Christians to understand, let alone convey to those hostile or disinterested or corrupted or misled. We are nevertheless a culture hungry for mercy, as audiences or readers so often testify in the very act of leaning closer to the stage, or weeping in a darkened theater, or telling a coworker, "You've just got to read this book!" Pictures of God's mercy—shown forth in the flesh of his followers or in the programs of his church or in the imaginative offerings of an artist— open opportunities for the gospel in this visual age, which is becoming increasingly image-dominated.

Our Image-Dominated Culture

Neal Postman, a communication theorist, says that we are becoming an image-dominated people. He concludes that because so much information is disseminated visually, the ways in which people receive truth are being dramatically altered. He writes:

> We have reached, I believe, a critical mass in that electronic media have decisively and irreversibly changed the character of our symbolic environment. We are now a culture whose information, ideas and epistemology are given form by television, not by the printed word.[12]

His astute analysis reinforces the idea that our increasingly visual culture must have pictures that clearly display qualities of God's nature in order to comprehend who he is, how he acts, and what he is like. Amy and Polly, frustrated in their attempts to describe the hospice hold, eventually resorted to a physical demonstration ("We'll just show you"). We need to be shown. For most, words are not enough.

If this is true, then the church must form pictures that convey our word-dominated theology. These are doors for the image-dominated person to enter, glimpses that can invite understanding. We can construct pictures in our modes of telling—in what we write, in how we teach, in the storytelling style of our ordinary conversations. Our very bodies, what Scripture calls "living sacrifices,"[13] can model what God is like in our daily occurrences, so our neighbors, our colleagues at work, the stranger in the marketplace, the traveler beside us in the airport, can see. We must not forget the opportunities for "showing forth."

Interestingly enough, the God of the Old Testament gave such pictures of himself to his prophets who were struggling to tell "the Word of the Lord" to an idol (image)-dominated culture. God gave a picture of mercy—and a prophetic showing of his Son—to the children of Israel, who were drawn to journey out of pagan, polytheistic Egypt into the purifying burning wilderness. This image was the ark of the covenant.

The lid of the ark was a gold slab on which two cherubs (winged lions with human heads) faced each other, their wings outspread. This was called the *mercy seat*. Within the ark itself were Aaron's rod, a pot of manna, and the two tables of the Law.[14]

The notes in my reference Bible read,

> The symbolism of the mercy seat surmounting the tables of the Law is representative of the covering of law by mercy. Thus it speaks of Christ and His perfect atonement which met the demands of the Law, making possible divine mercy. The mercy seat is a type of Christ. Once a year the high priest came with blood to make atonement for his sins and the sins of the

people. At the mercy seat God met and communed with those who came through blood. All believers now have access to the mercy seat through Christ, their High Priest.[15]

We would probably be surprised by the number of times we can be symbols of mercy to our friends.

THE ROUNDING CIRCLE, A MERCY SEAT

A woman came into my life with multiple perplexities. Over the span of a year and a half, before she moved into a live-in treatment program, I was intimately involved in her life. Savvy enough by now to know that it takes a team of lay caregivers to work with extremely fractured psyches, a group of us formed to collaborate with the professionals who were committed to her health and healing. Due to the complex nature of her condition, I also conducted a review of the literature, as well as put myself under the informal supervision of a nationally known Christian psychologist who specialized in my friend's disorder. Even with all this support in place, our work of practical love was hard going.

To complicate matters, this woman was struggling to care for her children. Believe me, this was a wrenching experience. The damage from their mother's frail condition manifested itself in anxiety symptoms.

The woman was often in our home and frequently spent the night in my daughter's former bedroom, though she didn't live with us. One evening two of her children were also visiting.

Bedtime. The children were bathed and snuggled in pajamas, and all four of us were tucked in the bed (the mother was almost as tiny as her offspring). My husband, David, who is a master with little children, passed by the door and stuck his head in to wish us good night. Now a whole repertoire of cartoon songs is at David's grasp due to a stack of records memorized when he was a child. These routines have often entertained our own brood. "My name is Daffy Duck—Henk! Henk!" he sang, using the hall as stage entrance. "Some people think I'm loony. I'm like an old pi-an-o. A little out of tune-y." Then he became Bugs Bunny and took a bow. And then Elmer Fudd. Needless to say, he was a big hit with many calls for encores.

The little boy, shy, liquid-brown eyes above soft round cheeks, lisped, "Mr. David to sweep wif me."

I watched my dignified husband pause, shrug—all that work downstairs waiting and the bed was full, and what about the propriety of it?—but still, the little boy. Well, there was nothing else to be done. The songs must go on. The back rubs. The bedtime routines. The children must be delivered safely to their dreams. David scooched on one far edge of the by-now very full three-quarter-size antique bed.

The little girl had a delightful expression. She called playground merry-go-rounds "rounding circles." I noted it because I thought it would make a wonderful phrase for a children's book that I was writing. Looking back I see that David and I were the rounding circle. (And, oh, if my husband only knew how beautiful he is when he puts aside reserve and bows before tenderness; and how beautiful to me.)

Later, once the little ones were asleep and the adults had crept carefully out of bed, my husband built a fire in our living room fireplace and finally escaped to the waiting work. The mother and I and another woman who lived with us at the time found wire coat hangers, raided a kitchen cupboard, and toasted marshmallows in the fire. We laughed and sang more old songs and told funny stories about our disabilities. (Well, they told stories: the I-can-top-you kind, the guess-what-other-terrible-thing-happened-to-me kind of tale. When those were done, they told funny stories about meeting me.)

And I realized then that one of the great gifts David and I can give is moments of unblemished memory: something in time that is not ruined or torn, ugly, or filled with terror. Moments to pull from the hidden chamber of the heart and savor. There are many things we cannot do; I have well learned how little I have to give in face of the world's need, but I can protect the moments and the people resident within them for brief but powerful times. Like the cherubim on the mercy seat, for some we are the rounding circle. We are pietàs.

In a sense, the mercy seat in the New Testament is Christ. Instead of a gold lid, we have a rough-hewn dirt hill: Golgotha. Instead of cherubim, we have two thieves. Instead of the blood of goats, we have the shed blood of the Beloved. He has become the propitiation for the sins of the world. And his arms are stretched wide. In the words of the Anglican prayer book, which worshipers repeat Sunday after Sunday throughout the year: "Christ, have mercy. Lord, have mercy." The church appeals to Mercy to cover it with mercy.

I remember that G. K. Chesterton once said something to the effect that children demand justice because they are innocent, but adults seek mercy because they are guilty. Christ taught his followers, who had received his mercy and watched him dispense it (like Father, like Son): "Blessed are the merciful, / For they shall obtain mercy."[16] The principle seems to work like this: We give mercy and receive it and give it again and receive it again.

Unfortunately, the church too often exercises judgment with little compassion. We are frighteningly like the character in Shakespeare's play *Coriolanus* about whom it was spoken: "There is no more mercy in him than there is milk in a male tiger."[17] Christ confronts judgment out of his own experiential understanding of the heavenly Father's nature, "But if you had known what this means, 'I desire mercy and not sacrifice,' you would not have condemned the guiltless."[18]

Standards of righteousness are important, but they should always be established within the context of grace. If not, authority will inevitably lean into judgment, legalism will gallop wild, and autocracy will gleefully wield abusive power.

Our world naturally tolerates calls for righteousness when they are surrounded by a context of long-suffering mercy. At a Washington, D.C., prayer breakfast, Mother Teresa scolded her American political audience for their pro-abortion policies: "You do not want these babies," she said. "Give them to me. I and my sisters want these babies."[19] All sat quietly before her chastisement because she and the Missionaries of Charity have so amply displayed the implications of loving-kindness. Even the newspapers that reported her speech were careful not to slant their copy scathingly.

And mercy must be available for all— even those who offend us with their sins—if it is to mirror the mercy of God. None have captured this more eloquently than Portia in her oft-quoted soliloquy to Shylock in Shakespeare's *The Merchant of Venice*. The first beautiful refrains are almost too familiar: "The quality of mercy is not strain'd, / It droppeth as the gentle rain from heaven / Upon the place beneath; it is twice blest, / It blesseth him that gives and him that takes."[20]

From that same play, these lines are an exquisite evocation of God's mercy, particularly in its relationship to the rule of kings (or to those in positions of authority):

> 'Tis mightiest in the mightiest: it becomes
> The throned monarch better than his crown;
> His sceptre shows the force of temporal power,
> The attribute to awe and majesty,
> Wherein doth sit the dread and fear of kings;
> But mercy is above this sceptred sway;
> It is enthroned in the hearts of kings
> It is an attribute to God himself;
> And earthly power doth then show likest God's
> When mercy seasons justice. Therefore, Jew,
> Though justice be thy plea, consider this,
> That in the course of justice, none of us
> Should see salvation: we do pray for mercy;
> And that same prayer doth teach us all to render
> The deeds of mercy.[21]

Holders form living pietàs, lap-type lamentations over the broken body in life's sorrows. These are the ones impelled by mercy, and their acts most brilliantly portray God's merciful lovingkindness in the world. Richard Attenborough, who narrates the video *Mother Teresa,* begins, "There's a light in this world, a healing spirit more powerful than any darkness we may encounter. We sometimes lose sight of this force where there is too much pain. Then suddenly the spiritual emerges through the lives of ordinary people who hear a call and answer in extraordinary ways."[22]

MERCY GIVES ALL

We can all be mercy-givers, with our own hospice holds. In thirty-five years of marriage, there have probably been only seven or eight years when David and I haven't had someone (other than our own four children) living with us. I am often asked, "How do these people find you?" And the answer is, I don't really know. Perhaps someone has left a chalk mark hidden outside our front door, pointing the way. I do know the ones I am supposed to take into our family life: They are those for whom I am suddenly filled with a rush of tender-loving mercy.

Some of these young adults are internationals or college students, some are friends of our children. Their stays vary from a few weeks to a couple of years, depending on their need for housing, for a family environment, for comfort or safety. Many have been severely wounded emotionally, and my gift of care or healing has been decidedly inadequate when compared to their pain. Undoubtedly, I have been the receiver. Knowing these who privilege us by living in our home has been a journey into courage; I have learned to admire what it has taken for them to stay alive.

My pains are minor in comparison. Because I have seen the results of destruction, I am just grateful for simple things: the sunshine, the wind in the trees, happy children. Through these guests' eyes and experiences I have caught shuddering glimpses of true evil—not just careless ill, but blatant perversion and its terrifying effects on the human soul. I have become psychologically literate because of many dialogues, and I have been forced to look honestly into the fallibilities of my own psyche. Humility has taught me that my help is often no help at all. ("Well, that makes you feel better, but it doesn't do anything for me!" instructed one live-in. She was right.) I've cleaned blood from slit wrists and bathroom walls, held those shrieking in psychotic episodes, conferred with psychiatrists, social workers, and ward nurses. I've stood appalled in the emergency room while the stomach of a friend was pumped because of an overdose of drugs in attempted suicide. I've failed miserably a hundred times but I am also aware that the little I've been able to do has been unaccountably multiplied in its effect. "You have to understand," two have told me, "I would not be alive today if you had not taken me into your home." Mercy, I believe, covers even our botched attempts.

Holding, in its physical or spiritual aspects, is one of the primary works of the church. And this is the meaning that all the pietàs lead me to. We must learn how to hold one another well, with mercy, because in doing this work, we do the work of God in the world. We hold when we take people into our embrace. We hold when we take people into our hearts. We hold when we take them into our schedules, our lives, our homes. We hold when we keep vigil with them in deathwatches. We hold when we take them into our prayers.

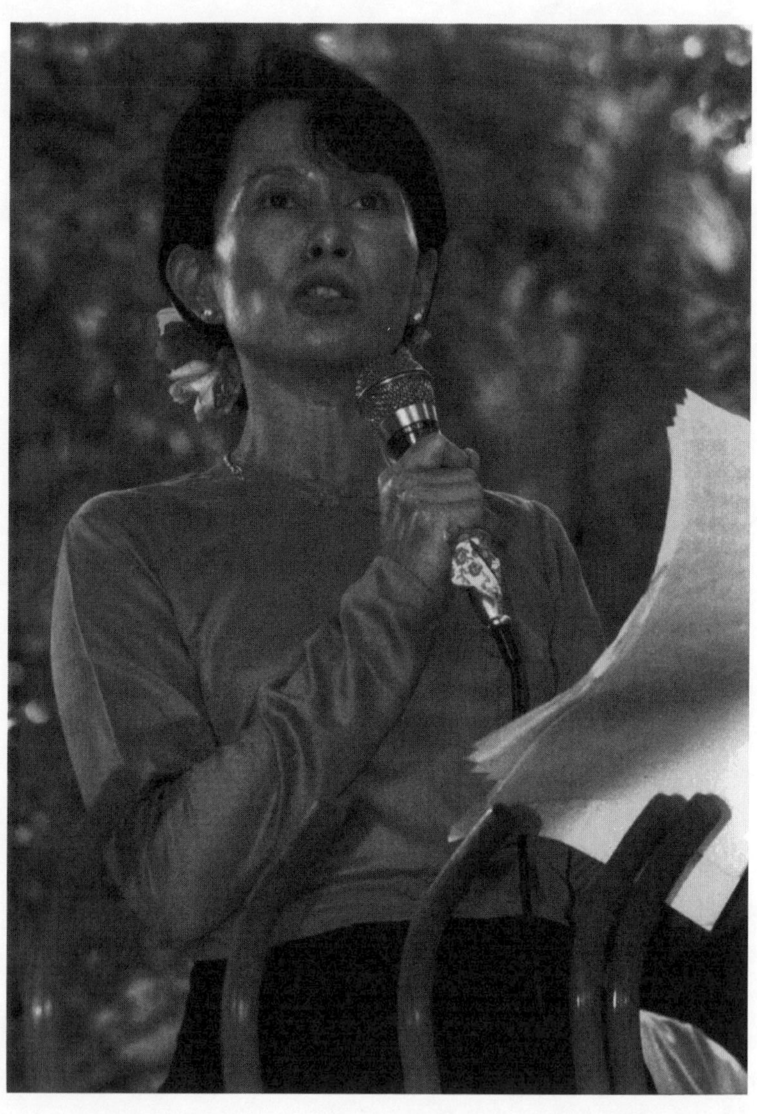

Aung San Suu Kyi, the human rights activist and leader of Burma's National League for Democracy (NLD) who was imprisoned for six years by the Burmese government, is a braveheart who understands about laying down her life for a larger cause. *Photo by AP/Wide World Photos*

Chapter Four

BRAVE HEARTS

During a retirement dinner for a mutual friend, the president emeritus of a large evangelical college and I were table companions; he was scheduled to deliver the evening address.

"What is your spiritual growth-edge?" I questioned, somewhere between the salad and the main course.

"Oh, Karen," he replied. "I think what I am learning most about is the Cross. You know we evangelicals don't like to think about the Cross very much. In our haste to get to the Resurrection we overlook the most central act of redemption."

During my past seasons of sorrows, I have (and am) seriously considering the Cross. This meditation has extended for years now, because minor crucifixions have continued, one after the other, without seeming end. I am discovering that it is the Cross itself that "holds" us during the suffering—the suffering that life devises and that God then uses for his own purpose, bringing amazing good to us and to others through us.

The Cross. Perhaps I have never understood this crucifixion, which is violently jammed into the living heart of Christendom. This shocking act of God, this paganlike sacrifice of a firstborn, which has been argued over, decried, declaimed, and denounced from the moment the Roman gibbet impaled the ground that all the witnesses call Golgotha. Why failure? Why this bloody deed? Why this nakedness and ignominy? Why this torn flesh and ugly torture?

Mel Gibson's Academy Award–winning film *Braveheart* captures something fresh about the Crucifixion that all the treatises written by sincere and seminary-educated theologians cannot. A cinematic treatment of the true story of the medieval Scots hero William Wallace, the film traces how he led a revolt against the occupying English and its monarch, King Edward I. The story of Wallace has stirred the national pride of Scotland's men and women for more than six hundred years.

Detractors are right in complaining that this film graphically depicts bloody medieval warfare. But as Michael Kilian, a Chicago newspaper critic, noted: "Gibson has created a brilliant portrayal of authentic history in terrible times, when most people went about filthy and in rags; lived in crude, infested, sopping sod hovels; bore the marks of ravaging diseases such as leprosy; and had to fight for their lives every day."[1]

According to *The Dictionary of National Biography,* the historical facts are these: In 1296 King Edward invaded Scotland, driving out the Scottish king and stationing English soldiers throughout the land. A patriot insurrection formed under the leadership of Wallace. In response, the English raised an army, which Wallace defeated at Stirling Point; then King Edward hurried home from France and led a larger, more heavily armored soldiery against the Scottish clansmen at Falkirk. There the Scots failed, and Wallace escaped to the mountains to carry on a resistance movement, only to be captured seven years later, due to betrayal in his own camp. He was tried and executed for treason.

The *Biography* gives a sensible assessment of Wallace's worth:

> In the records of Scotland and England and in the contemporary chronicles he stands out boldly as the chief champion of the Scottish nation in the struggle for independence, and the chief enemy of Edward in the premature attempt to unite Britain under one scepter. His name has become one of the great names of history. He was a general who knew how to discipline men and to rouse their enthusiasm; a statesman, if we may trust indications few but pregnant, who, had more time been granted and better support given him by the nobles, might have restored a nation and created a state.[2]

What I find remarkable in *Braveheart* is its legendary motif of the redeemer/liberator. A personal list of my contemporary heroes shows me that I am drawn to those individuals with courage enough to challenge the systemic oppressions of their cultures. Few, in fact, survive the challenge. The assassin lurks, prison waits, military dictatorships are patient only so long. So I consider it superhumanly remarkable that people like Nelson Mandela even survive, let alone live long enough to lead a coalition that dismantles South Africa's entrenched apartheid.

Currently I am watching the life of Aung San Suu Kyi, the human rights activist and leader of Burma's National League for

Democracy (NLD), who was released from six years of house arrest by the military junta. She is the daughter of Burma's national hero, Aung San, who, with his cabinet, was machine-gunned to death when she was two years old, just before Burma gained the independence to which he had dedicated his life. Despite her house arrest, which began in July 1989 and ended in July 1995, the NLD party she founded went on to win an overwhelming electoral victory in May of 1990, securing nearly 80 percent of the vote (and was then quickly dismantled by the dictatorship, which reacted by throwing most of the NLD officers and supporters into jail or driving them into exile).

Aung San Suu Kyi was thrust into the political furor when she returned home to help her ailing mother during the summer of 1988. Having left Burma at the age of fifteen when her widowed mother was appointed ambassador to India, she studied abroad, married a British scholar, and eventually settled in England. Her arrival home to Burma occurred on the heels of nationwide antigovernment protests, which began at the announcement of the retirement of Ne Win, the country's longtime strongman, and exploded when the jubilant street celebrations were met by troops with guns. Casualties mounted and the demonstrators grew until they numbered in the hundreds of thousands. The brutal clampdown by the military (in one incident forty-one students suffocated to death in a police van) and the massacre of civilians propelled Aung San Suu Kyi into action. The protests continued (joined by Buddhist nuns, housewives, and students banging their pots and pans), as the Burmese people demonstrated noisily for human rights. In August of 1988, she spoke to a throng of five hundred thousand on the slopes beneath Shwedagon Pagoda near the center of Rangoon.

Calling for reasonable dialogue and insisting on the moral imperatives of peaceable resistance, Aung San Suu Kyi defied the junta's ban on peaceful demonstrations, crisscrossing Burma in campaigns that drew thousands of sympathetic Burmese supporters. On one occasion, an army captain halted Aung San Suu Kyi and her campaigners at gunpoint, threatening to open fire if they advanced. Motioning her supporters to step aside, she deliberately walked alone down the road into the line of the military roadblock, quickly deciding that only one life should be put at risk, and that life was hers. At the last moment, a major on the sidelines contravened the order.

Even though she was separated from her husband and two sons, whose passports and visas were revoked for years, she refused to capitulate to the demands of the SLORC (State Law and Order Restoration Council). While still under detainment, she was awarded the Sakharov Prize for Freedom of Thought by the European Parliament, the Thorolf Rafto Prize for Human Rights, and in 1991, the Nobel Peace Prize. During these years Aung San Suu Kyi became a legend in the minds of her countrymen. Friends and foes alike call her "The Lady." It remains to be seen how history will use her.

These remarkable liberators hold to common understandings that model profound realities for the rest of us. They know that one must let loose of what one holds most dear in order to gain what is best for the whole. They know they must not be afraid to lay down their lives for the success of larger causes.

"It is not power that corrupts," writes Aung San, "but fear. Fear of losing power corrupts those who wield it and fear of the scourge of power corrupts those who are subject to it. . . . Saints, it has been said, are the sinners who go on trying. So free men are the oppressed who go on trying and who in the process make themselves fit to bear the responsibilities and to uphold the disciplines which will maintain a free society. Among the basic freedoms to which men aspire that their lives might be full and uncramped, freedom from fear stands out as both a means and an end."[3]

Christ, of course, is the supreme liberator, striking at the very core of the oppressions that bind us to our worst selves, which then interweave outward into overarching societal woes. Christ mounts a resistance campaign that attempts to free us from the great oppressor: our own twisted, bent beings. He died so that a transformation could occur within. His is not a political salvation because the profound truth is this: Until we are delivered from our own sinful cores, we will corrupt all societal units, be it our families, churches, towns, nations, or global communities.

The theologian Reinhold Niebuhr remarked a generation ago that no amount of contrary evidence seems to disturb humanity's good opinion of itself. Atrocities. Genocide. Violence. Rapaciousness. History has proven that the fallen heart will only express itself, ultimately, in a fallen way. Incapable of transforming ourselves, we humans must be supernaturally transformed.

Stories of the lives of people like William Wallace and Aung San Suu Kyi give us courageous examples to follow. On a very small scale I have had opportunity during the last few years to observe the meaning of integrity from those who have modeled it to me in my own crisis. Of course, I do not in any way consider these past years to compare with the magnitude of those heroic individuals who have been forced to function grandly on national or international platforms. But personal experience often affords us certain realities out of which we can expand some understanding, however meager, of broader realities.

MODELS OF INTEGRITY

During the writing of *Lonely No More*, I became aware of a crossroads decision facing me; it was the classic midlife question: What was I going to do with the rest of the life God gave me? If I was going to be a writer, then I needed to concentrate completely on framing a writer's life, without the large amounts of diversions I had juggled for all of my married life. Fast on the heels of this perplexity came other considerations: If I were going to frame a writer's life, what would that look like? What further education would it require? What would I have to sacrifice in order to write well? And ultimately, was I a good enough writer to even justify such a drastic trimming?

Interestingly enough, my body assisted me in coming to some conclusions. I began to develop allergic reactions to all the travel required by conference speaking: breathing the recycled airplane air, crossing ecological zones, pogo-sticking from one season into another and then back again. All this set off a chronic hacking cough, with irritating and constant sinus drainage that required vast supplies of over-the-counter medication to control. My physiological system was obviously screaming, "Enough!"

So I began to refuse invitations (working two years out), and by the time the controversy hit regarding my book, only eight engagements remained on my speaking calendar. Four of these were canceled on me, while four remained firm; and in this (admittedly, a trial of humiliation at the time) there was a world of learning. I want to be careful not to negate the planners who uninvited me (or the authorities who insisted that the planners do so), nor do I deny their prerogatives to make a judgment call regarding their own conferences and retreats.

But I would much rather look to the example set for me by people who stood beside me in the controversy and decided to continue as planned with our contracted agreements. I continually found myself asking, *Would I have done the same under a set of similar circumstances?*

Scheduled to speak for a denominational women's retreat—meeting number seven—(Oh, how glad I would be when my commitments were finally finished!), I received a phone call from the district superintendent of that region, the gist of which I remember to have gone as follows:

"Karen," he said, "we've been having some interesting meetings out here."

Uh-oh. I thought I knew what was coming.

"As you know," he continued, "there has been controversy surrounding your book and you and your husband's ministry. Several folk from this area have met with me, asking that we cancel you for our upcoming retreat."

"I am so sorry," I replied. "The last thing I want to do is add to the workload of a person such as yourself."

"No. That's all right. I actually feel like this has been a very good lesson in coming to terms with what it means to disagree but still exercise charity and to develop tolerance in diversity. But, you're right. It has taken a lot of time."

He continued, "I think we've settled things, for the most part. But I also didn't think it was fair for you to come here without knowing that some people, a small but vocal group, are in disagreement with you."

"Will it be counterproductive if I speak? Should I not come?"

"Oh, no. No. No. That would be exactly what we should *not* do right now. You need to know that I read your book. In fact, I read all of it. And I had to tell these folk that I actually liked the book and found nothing scripturally unsound about it. Because of reading it, there were even things I needed to rethink regarding my own patterns of overwork."

I was more than slightly amazed.

A few moments later, I asked, "Why didn't you just cancel me when all of this happened? You had time, certainly. Wouldn't it have been a lot easier?"

"Well," he replied, and in this was the greatest lesson for me, "we felt that it was a matter of integrity. You and David have ministered publicly for decades. I believe it would be morally wrong to bow before this little storm of controversy. At this time, more than ever, you need other leaders to stand beside you. And that is what we are going to do. We believe in you."

I do not know if under similar circumstances in this man's position I would have been as stalwart.

Through all my small season of sorrows, I've often thought about the axiom, When good men remain silent, evil men prevail. Again, I want to be clearly understood: These thoughts have not been in regard to my critics, nor toward those poor folk with hundreds of people registered to attend a conference they have planned where the scheduled speaker has suddenly become an object of controversy. That storm can be very disorienting, as I well know. I am primarily concerned to examine myself: How do I stand firm in matters of personal integrity and in my minor role in Christendom?

This personal experience has taught me that many of us, passionately Christian in declaration, nevertheless function out of a reactionary self-protective position when faced with a crisis of disagreeable circumstances. Most tended to ask: What kind of hot water is the Mainses' predicament going to put me into with my constituencies? rather than, What are the scriptural parameters that bear on this situation? Ironically, the people who were the least biblical in their actions were often the ones most insistent that I was not biblical in my writing.

I think the axiom for me is not so much, When good men remain silent, evil men prevail, as When good men and women remain silent, other good men and women slip and slide.

Truthfully, I have met many good folk in the past few years. They have stood beside me and held me. Humiliation has been forced upon me at the hands of my critics, but true humbleness, and the strength to maintain it, has come to me from those people of principle who know how to stand firm. I could name them, but their personal integrity is such that my naming them would probably be a source of deep embarrassment. So all I will say is that each one, each man and woman, has taught me great lessons about moral courage. In mercy, in charity, and in truth, they formed a pietà around me in which I have rested while the pain did its work. They are my heroes and heroines and they have lifted me when I was weak, confused, distressed. May God's richest blessing be upon them. In my world, these are the ones with brave hearts. May I learn to emulate their integrity.

Cry Freedom

The cinematic moment in *Braveheart* that forced me to think again about the Crucifixion was the closing scene of Wallace's torture and execution. The film actually spares us some of the gruesomeness of the historical reality. In the public square Wallace, with the instruments for dissection in front of him, refuses to confess his treason (having never taken an oath of fealty to the king, he maintains he is not legally guilty of treason), nor to pledge allegiance to the English monarchy, nor to cry for mercy in exchange for an easy death, beheading. Spread on his back in the form of crucifixion, awaiting disemboweling, Wallace is asked one last time by the executioner if he will beg for mercy. Wallace throws back his head, gathers what remaining strength is left, and bellows out instead, "Freeeeeedom!"

Randall Wallace, a descendant and the author of the historical novel upon which the film is based, writes, "The shout rang through the town. Hamish, Stephen, everyone, on the square, heard it. The princess heard it at her open window. Longshanks and his son seemed to hear. The cry echoed as if the wind could carry it through the ends of Scotland; and Robert the Bruce, on the walls of his castle, looked up sharply as if he too had heard."[4]

Admittedly, this is a literary conceit—the author is exercising imaginative liberties—but the reader (or viewer) is nevertheless tempted to want the very currents of the earth's air to carry this hero's death-cry of defiance throughout the land.

The broken, dismembered body of Wallace, which was delivered to the four corners of Britain as a horrific warning, had the opposite effect to what King Edward intended. The Scots clansmen, this time backed by a united nobility, began to raise a determined rebellion, led by Robert the Bruce. In 1314, just nine years after Wallace's execution, some forty thousand Scots faced sixty thousand English soldiers at Bannockburn. By fighting from a superior position—they dug pits that stopped the advancing enemy along their line of attack—the Scottish finally won their country's independence, leaving ten thousand English dead on the field to four thousand Scottish losses. In the film, a war cry goes up from the defending forces before the battle: "Wal-lace! Wal-lace! Wal-lace! Wal-lace!" (Cinematic fantasy, perhaps, but extremely satisfying fantasy for the stuff of legends.)

Who knows what the Scots clansmen really cried before that battle. In his poem "Bruce to His Men at Bannockburn," Robert Burns, the great national poet, penned the famous line, "Scots, wha hae wi' Wallace bled." No matter the particulars, history shows these warriors certainly finished what their countrymen began.

Christ, the supreme liberator of souls, cried a shout of freedom at the last moments of his torture: "It is finished!" John, in his gospel, is the only apostle who records these exact words. Chapter 19, verse 28, mentions that Jesus said, "I thirst!" A bowlful of sour wine was offered with a hyssop straw in a sponge. "So when Jesus had received the sour wine, He said, 'It is finished!' And bowing His head, He gave up His spirit" (v. 30). This account sounds like the suffering resignation of One who has endured torture enough.

The other histories, those of Matthew, Mark, and Luke, do not record the words "It is finished!" among the final pronouncements of Christ, but two refer to the offering of the vinegar for thirst and the third mentions Christ taking his last breath. All three gospel writers, however, leave an extremely dramatic record of these last moments at the Cross. Records Matthew:

> And Jesus cried out again with a loud voice, and yielded up His spirit. Then, behold, the veil of the temple was torn in two from top to bottom; and the earth quaked, and the rocks were split, and the graves were opened; and many bodies of the saints who had fallen asleep were raised; and coming out of the graves after His resurrection, they went into the holy city and appeared to many.[5]

Mark's record is shorter, but similar:

> And Jesus cried out with a loud voice, and breathed His last. Then the veil of the temple was torn in two from top to bottom. So when the centurion, who stood opposite Him, saw that He cried out like this and breathed His last, he said, "Truly this Man was the Son of God!"[6]

Luke, summarizing eyewitness accounts years later, records:

> And when Jesus had cried out with a loud voice, He said, "Father, into Your hands I commit My spirit." Having said this, He breathed His last. So when the centurion saw what had happened, he glorified God, saying, "Certainly this was a righteous Man!"[7]

The variations in these texts are actually proof to me of their authenticity. There is nothing essentially contradictory here. Any investigating reporter, gathering eyewitness accounts after a tragedy or a natural disaster, knows that a comprehensive "whole" story will only be obtained by collecting and collating a multitude of seemingly disparate pieces. I would distrust the Gospel narratives if they read like copyists' manuscripts. This point of view, that point of view, the edges not quite fitting—this means that real people, telling about a remarkable event, honestly portrayed what they saw and remembered.

Certainly then, a comparison of the four accounts of Christ's death do not prohibit the interpretation that "It is finished!" was something akin to Wallace gathering his last breath to bellow "Freedom!" A "victim redeemer" is just not to be found in these records. Jesus, the spiritual insurrectionist, orchestrated the timing of his torture and death; he set off the very controversies he knew would incite the crowds to laud him and the Jewish leaders to scheme his execution; he maintained utter control over himself during unspeakable shame and suffering; in deliberate fashion, he fulfilled Old Testament prophecies; he even offered compassion to those watching him die.

Then, just as this dramatic masterwork rolls into the final act, Christ lifts his head and shouts, "Finished! [Freedom!]" The earth shakes. No literary conceit here, but a redemptive drama of the highest divine order.

The film *Braveheart* gave me a visual image against which to crunch the overly familiar account. In addition, I must understand that the minor crucifixions that occur in my own journey, despite my repugnance at them, can be events of liberation.

Unpleasant tortures beyond my control (but used by God, and anything can be used by him) can free me from my clutching onto my self. Søren Kierkegaard wrote, "God creates everything out of nothing—and everything which God is to use he first reduces to nothing."[8]

All the spiritual writings of any depth tell of this necessary demolition of our selfish fixations. Tozer emphasized his need to be freed from the "fine threads of the self-life, the hyphenated sins of the human spirit; self-sufficiency, self-pity, self-absorption, self-abuse, self-aggrandizement, self-castigation, self-deception, self-exaltation, self-depreciation, self-indulgence, self-hatred, etc., etc."[9]

Wooden Stakes

There is a rage these days for vampire lore. Pulp fiction, best-selling books, and Hollywood movies concentrate on these blood-lusting figures of darkness. A young friend, having turned his back on faith, had been reading these chronicles, so I picked up a copy of one of the more popular works and was so repelled by the ghoulish fixation on death and killing that my revulsion prevented me from finishing it.

I wish I were as repelled by my own self-indulgences, the vampirelike darkness that feeds itself on my own lurking errors, sucking and growing, hiding the beauties of Christ from blazing forth within me. Part of vampire lore maintains that only a wooden stake driven through the heart can end the immortal existence of these evil creatures. In a sense, a stake must be driven through the core of our *own* self-deceived centers in order for us to experience the deconstruction of our conniving self-drives.

The Cross. "I have been crucified with Christ . . ." cried the apostle Paul.[10]

Heaven knows, these works of crucifixion that ultimately free us to true life are not sought. Nor can I orchestrate them. Left to my own devices, I will conduct Calvary in my own self-interest, for the sake of displaying to others that I have done so, and thereby winning their approval. Such false humility is a blight on Christendom and characterizes too many of its leaders. It is a horror that leers at me. Thomas Merton wrote, "He thinks his own pride is the Holy Ghost. . . . This sickness is most dangerous when it succeeds in looking like humility. When a proud man thinks he is humble, his case is hopeless."[11]

No. No, this must be a work of God, contrived by him, in his own timing and in his own way. My role, as I am instructed by the many who have gone before me, is to bow, to accept that this painful agony will be made into a good thing, to surrender to the perfect working of the will of my Maker though I cannot see the outcome. My role is to surrender and not fight against the wooden stake being pounded into the arrogance, the pettiness, the narcissism, the concentration upon my own achievements and abilities. My role is to pray, "Empty me. Empty me even of life if that is the way you can work your work in your way. I choose to trust that your plan for me is good."

All of us, if we are to truly follow in the Christ-way, must have courage, must become bravehearts. This can happen if we understand well how death-cries can become cries of freedom. And it is at the point where we accept the benefits that crucifixions bring into our lives that holding lessons can begin.

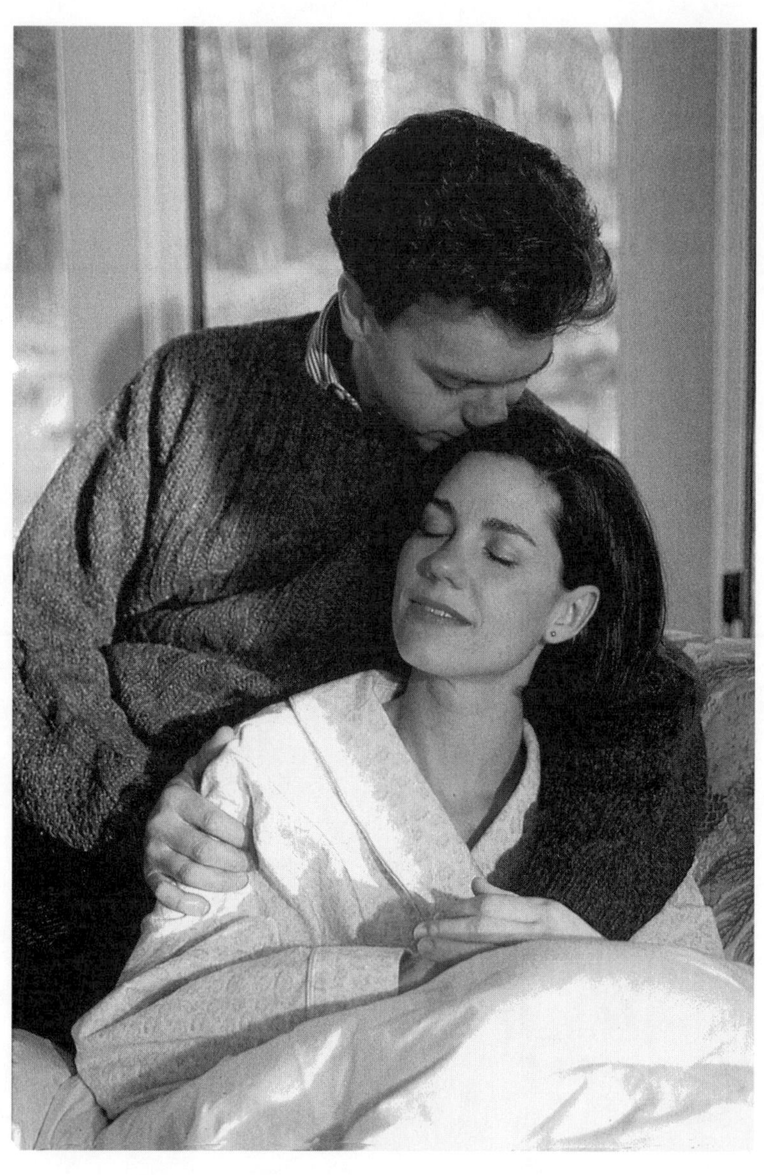

There is power in touch. It can heal, it can love, it can show mercy. This is the first holding lesson. *Photo courtesy of Superstock*

Chapter Five

HOLDING LESSONS

Anne Lamott is a writer whose originality of language often challenges me into thinking freshly about the creative process. *Operating Instructions: A Journal of My Son's First Year* introduced me to her work. In it, she records the trials of raising her child without a father, but she also highlights the poignancy of helpers and the flowering of what she calls her "shabby faith." Her irreverencies would certainly offend some Christians, but paradoxically, they are the very idioms that make her spiritual birth relevant to the secular reader. And her provocative views and outrageous descriptions frequently cause me to howl with laughter: "Almost all my close friends are walking personality disorders," she writes.[1]

Mostly what I like in Lamott is her authentic journey toward Christian meaning:

> I know that it is odd to a lot of people that I am religious—I mean, it's odd to me that I'm religious, I never meant to be. I don't quite know how it happened: I think that at some point, a long time ago, I made a decision to believe, and then every step of the way, even through the worst of it . . . I could feel the presence of something I could turn to . . . that Jesus is there with us everyplace Sam and I go.[2]

Because she is so transparently needy (one reviewer commended her understanding of "ordinary madness"), her books deal with themes such as human encouragement and support.

One story Lamott tells is about a writer friend who puts her toddler to rest in a shade-darkened room, then goes off to write. In a little while, she hears knocking and discovers that her son has crawled out of his playpen and has somehow locked the door. He is calling for help, "Mommy! Mommy!"

> "Jiggle the doorknob, darling," and of course he didn't speak much English—mostly he seemed to speak Urdu. After a moment, it became clear to him that his mother couldn't open the door, and the panic set in. He began sobbing. . . . And there he was in the dark, this terrified little child. Finally she did the only thing she could, which was to slide her fingers underneath the door, where there was a one-inch space. . . . So they stayed like that for a really long time, on the floor, him holding onto her fingers in the dark. He stopped crying. She kept wanting to go call the fire department or something, but she felt that contact was the most important thing.[3]

Eventually, after several tries, the child jiggled the doorknob again and the lock popped open. Lamott draws parallels from this incident to her own relationship with God, but for me, this story is the place to begin holding lessons. Holding will involve touch on some level.

We are going to have to learn the importance of touch, as well as its dangers; then learn how, as agents of mercy, to hold others well.

I have learned five lessons to help me do this. We will look at them in the next three chapters. The first holding lesson examines the healing power of touch.

Touch Is Important
(It Can Heal)

D. W. Winnicott, a famous British psychiatrist and pediatrician, coined the phrase "the maternal mode," which became a well-known psychiatric term. It describes the basic security a person experiences in childhood from the most important early figure in his or her life: the mother. In fact, children with no apparent medical condition may decline in health, suffer physically, and even die in the condition known as the failure-to-thrive syndrome. The deterioration is due to severe deprivation: There simply is no one to hold or touch them.

"Rub my back, Mommy," my children used to intone when they were small. And I would tease, echoing their supplications, "Rub my back! You're always wanting a back rub." Their pleas were accompanied by what in our home is dubbed "the poor, pitiful person" look. But eventually, the back would get rubbed, and we would talk about the day and child-size ideas and the events and happenings of their worlds—and God. (God always seemed to slip into these drifting-into-sleep moments.) Calm descended. Quiet. Peace.

One of my sons, while in grade school, introduced the hand massage (or as termed in family pig latin, "anday-hay, assagay-may"). The cure for stomachaches, crankiness, restlessness in church, childhood emotional distresses. "You massage my hand for ten minutes and I'll massage yours." The ubiquitous deal. Then hand massages evolved into a business proposition: ten minutes for thirty-five cents. A steal, except that I nodded off after the first four minutes, so relaxed did I become. My son proved to be the more canny financier.

One of the women who lived with us had spent ten years on the streets of Atlanta and, consequently, struggled with sleep disorders. Touch, with all its negative sexual connotations and violent intentions, was not trusted. We discovered, however, that when I extended the family custom of massaging her hand—gently pressing the pad of the palm, stretching the fingers out and back, putting pressure on the wrist, skimming the skin with light, fluttering taps—she instantly relaxed. It was amazing to the point of being funny. Apply gentle pressure, then release, apply gentle pressure, then release.

Inevitably, a transmutation would occur beneath my hands, before my eyes. My friend would slip into the closest semblance of a purring cat that I'd ever seen. Sometimes I would pull her up from the couch to send her to bed. Her muscles had become so at ease that she couldn't push out of it on her own. Like Temple Grandin, my housemate, usually tough, uptight, and on guard, became gentle, soft-spoken, and sleepy, her whole being sinking into some sort of great physiological sigh.

Modern research reveals that when premature infants are given short daily massages, their growth rate is increased by nearly 50 percent. Laboratory studies conducted by the Touch Research Institute at the University of Miami School of Medicine show that baby mice deprived of touch actually suffer a decrease in the amount of the gene necessary to promote growth.[4]

In another study the Touch Institute discovered that when parents of diabetic children gave nightly massages, both the parents and the children had less anxiety and depression; in addition, the physiological effect also dramatically lowered the children's blood-glucose levels to normal range. Long-term improvements were also experienced by thirty patients suffering from fibromyalgia, a disorder involving generalized body pain with much accompanying discomfort. Massages, given twice a week for five weeks, resulted in less pain, reduced stiffness and fatigue, and better sleep. Asthmatic children, administered nightly bedtime rubs, experienced better breathing and fewer asthma attacks.[5] And what about Temple Grandin's squeeze machine and other studies on autistic children, most of whom are actually bothered by touch? Regular, predictable massages, administered over a month, resulted in less distraction, more attention, and more social connectedness. The most common finding in the Touch Institute's studies was that massage reduced stress (notably through reducing the hormones that detrimentally affect our physical systems) and lowered levels of anxiety and depression.[6]

Any good mother (or good father) knows the importance of touch. We hold, we bounce little bodies going ripe with sleep on our shoulders, we calm our children's restlessness by running our fingers through their hair, we settle anxieties by patting.

"There, there. Now, now," we say to the weeping child. "It will be better." All the while, almost unconsciously, the contact goes on. Our touch soothes, wipes tears, strokes the face, presses the child close. The touch of a good father, of a good mother, is a model we can keep in mind.

Most intriguing to me is that both the giver and the receiver benefit from healthy touch. In one study, elderly people who gave back rubs to children in an orphanage improved so much themselves, they required less medical attention from their own doctors.[7] And a pet for the elderly provides similar results: a live animal to stroke seems to work reciprocal benefits.[8] I'm intrigued to ponder what instinct propelled the begging of my own children, "Rub my back, Mommy. Rub my back." And what kind of gifts were unknowingly exchanged?

If we are going to plumb the depths of our holding lessons, we must begin with the understanding that holding and being held, giving and receiving safe, tender, protective touch is one of the basic needs of human existence. It is indeed, as the studies show, essential to growth, to survival, to well-being. Nature itself gives us endless pictures of this dynamic. Biologists speak of *tropisms* (the orientation of an organism to grow in response to an external stimulus): the roots of a plant stretch down into the soil while its branches above seek light. Scientists speak of *tactisms* (growth that comes when two organisms bend toward one another): the life-prolonging fusion of the paramecia or the curling tucked forms of two seals on a rocky shore on the Galápagos Islands. (Amy Harwell, my friend who had cancer, showed me a black-and-white photo of two sea lions curled together, which she had photographed herself while vacationing—a trip at the top of her BID list [things to do Before I Die].)

Touching, or holding, finds expression in a broad range of variables. The fleeting brush of fingers on another's sleeve. The sacramental laying on of hands. The profound steadying that occurs when friends stand strong beside us at our moments of greatest pain. Holding can be that unseen community of witnesses who conduct the work of intercessory prayer, bringing before the throne of God the mighty distresses of Christ's body; or it can be the grandchild who, when our hearts are burdened beyond bearing, climbs into our lap and falls asleep in our arms. And then we, too, slip into rest.

The deepest meaning of touching or holding is its potential sacramentally; touch has the power to convey something of God through a very human means. This is an essential message of the Incarnation: Christ took on flesh to make God knowable; we, filled with the Spirit of this Christ, can do the same. In a sense, if I am to learn the holding lessons well, I must stand aside, put my ego (which is always seeking to impress or to feel itself essential in the eyes of others) behind me and simply *be there*, quietly.

My focus is not particularly on the results but on whether the quality of mercy I give is truly Christlike. Do I listen deeply? Do I allow myself to see the beauty of the personality before me? Do I seek to see in others the same potential that God sees? Do I speak aloud the words that name that beauty and potential? Am I tenderhearted? The results, whatever they may be, are out of my power to control.

Don Allender writes in *Bold Love,* "The two central passions of the heart are a desire for connection that does not consume or destroy the other (is not dependent and weak) and a hunger for impact that leads to greater beauty and justice. Connection, or love, is experienced in countless ways, but we can synthesize the multifaceted elements of love with the word tenderness."[9]

Connection of any kind can be a form of holding. When a child is locked in the dark, terrified that no one can reach him, sometimes just the fingers touching beneath the door (or if we are the child, the voice of a kind friend over the phone, a note in the mail, time out for lunch together, a brief chat in the living room) is enough to ward off terror. Like the intuitive understanding of the mother, down on the floor, reassuring her weeping child on the other side of the shut door, we too need to operate from the conviction that "contact is the most important thing."

How unfortunate that we live in a society where touch is often violent, associated with sexual molestation or considered sissified or intrusive. One of the very things we need in order to be healthy is being denied to us by our technologically driven, increasingly suspicious, and often inhumane culture.

Unfortunately touch has not been a blessing to some.

Hazardous Touch

Undoubtedly, holding is risky. It can be offered inappropriately. It can offend. It can become loaded with sexual connotations, with cross-gender or same-gender enticements. Some people cannot bear to be touched. Touching can evoke the terror of past violent hands.

The sexualization of our culture and its brutality have made innocent touch suspect. Placards on the dangers of child sexual abuse are posted outside Sunday school classrooms in church hallways. We all know of pastors or have heard about ones who have fallen into sexual liaisons with parishioners. Ministering professionals are just coming to terms with the fact that the weeping woman sitting in their office with her story about a battering husband (so charming in congregational social affairs) is probably telling the truth, and indeed, she is coping with a life-risk environment that demands immediate intervention. Because there are pedophiles on the loose, teachers throughout the country are having to tell children about Good Touch/Bad Touch. Innocence is a dangerous alternative. The brutalization of our citizenry is an actuality.

In this environment, touch can be hazardous. It may be misread. In order to avoid difficulties, we may be tempted to rush to extreme conclusions. Draw a line in the sand: No Touching. No Holding. This measure, of course, creates exactly the opposite effect from what is intended; to forbid touch is a reverse form of brutalization in that it creates its own powerful deprivations.

In a culture where touch is suspect, the starvation for holding becomes enormous (people speak of "skin hunger"). In addition, such a society will not develop pictures of what healthy and appropriate touch looks like, so it will be in danger of losing the lore of touch that is taught by the good grandfather taking a child on his knee. The loving teacher who communicates her favor by word as well as by a pat on the back. A hand clasp that lasts a moment longer and says, "I'm really proud of you." Friends who hug on meeting or throw their arms around one another's shoulders while walking. The father who play-wrestles regularly with his boys and girls. The camaraderie of the sports team with their comfortable familiarity: the butt-pat, the leaping on one another after a goal, the locker room do-well slaps.

Let us not lose the lore of touching, but learn instead to set holding within its appropriate parameters. For some, positive touch is as natural as breathing; for others it is an acquired ability. But all of us can learn to develop more of a capacity to give the kind of holding that sustains, strengthens, goes beyond its human meaning, and becomes a gift that has spiritual implications. We can learn to be proficient in our capacities for lap-type lamentations.

Touch is important. (It can heal.) And a second holding lesson is, Of course we are going to make mistakes.

We Are Going to Make Mistakes (But We Can Learn from Them)

My walking partner, Scottie May, is a Christian education consultant with a Ph.D. in that field of study. She kindly endures my ongoing, up-to-the-minute reports of writing agonies as I verbally wind my way through the difficulties of the latest project. The Prairie Path, miles of former railway easement restored for walkers here in the western suburbs of Chicago, has been the scene of many discussions on book content. One day as we were walking and talking together about the nuances of holding, she recalled an incident long ago as a young student nurse rotating through intensive care.

On an evening shift, she was assigned to a critically injured young man the same age as her fiancé. Unresponsive from massive head injuries sustained in an automobile accident, he nevertheless moaned frequently and gave physical indications of agitation. Drawn to his side, she spent long hours there, holding his hand, which he would squeeze intermittently with a vise-like grip.

She confessed, "I didn't know how to help him. It's intriguing that some experiences stand out in memory with heightened clarity. They're probably seminal in their meaning. This is one."

"What would you have done differently if you'd had more nursing wisdom?" I asked.

"Oh, I would have given more active comfort. I would have talked to him, told him what had happened, where he was. I would have made more physical contact. I might even have sung to him. I simply didn't have the experience yet. I wish I had realized that his agitation was more than just physical suffering. He was afraid, and I needed to do all within my power to comfort him. Gradually, I felt his grip lessen. He died while holding my hand."

We will make mistakes in these merciful attempts to hold people in life's sorrows. But we can learn from our mistakes how to become wise givers of mercy. God has promised, "If any of you lacks wisdom, let him ask of God, who gives to all liberally and without reproach, and it will be given to him."[10] One of the primary roles of the Holy Spirit is to lead us into all truth. The essential lifetime attitude we must maintain is that of a humble learner. I cannot overemphasize the importance of this: No matter how much we achieve in the area of knowledge, we are always novices in comparison to the vast universe of what there is to be learned. We will ever be just at the beginning.

One of the most helpful ministering principles I have discovered in a lifetime of people care is paradoxical: I am not nearly as important as I think I am, but I am much more important than I know. I remind myself of this complimentary contradiction whenever too much gladness at work well done (the stand up and crow over myself kind) rises in my soul.

The Paradoxical Principle

Sooner or later, pride will come slithering and curl at my feet, hissing, *Hey! You're good. You're really good*. The truth is, I am not nearly as important as I think I am. But I am much more important than I know.

This truth has salvaged me from many ravages of the tempter's bite, the venom that paralyzes my humility with the smug thoughts: *I'm special. I'm gifted. No one else can do the things I do.*

Several years ago, I was invited to speak at the closing banquet of the Christian Association for Psychological Studies annual convention. As these things often go, the dinner program, which included introductions and award presentations, ran over schedule, and I sat at the speaker's table in an increasingly stressed inward state, incrementally editing my speech from forty-five minutes to thirty-five minutes, then from thirty-five minutes to twenty-five, maybe twenty. Slash. Cut. Snip.

Looking out over the sea of faces, I became intensely aware that most were professionals with thousands more years of training and clinical experience than I. The preceding days had been jammed for them— either teaching or attending workshops and academic sessions. Yawns in the banquet room attested to brain fatigue. And now the dinner program was running long. I knew they'd all give anything to hear a humorist like Erma Bombeck rather than a psychological novice such as Karen Mains.

Fortunately, I had sense enough not to try to impress. Folly! screamed all the warning signs along that path. And when I finally did get to the podium, I guessed I could hold their attention for about twenty-five minutes max, and that only if I was very energetic. Common sense coached me to admit aloud that I was not a professional, that I hadn't really prepared a speech, so much as strung together a few stories out of my own life in ministry. "I have, however, learned a few things in these years of giving care to others. Perhaps these lessons will aid you. Perhaps you've already learned them. Just take or leave what I have to say."

The first lesson I presented was the paradoxical truth that *I am not nearly as important as I think I am, but I am much more important than I know.* Actually, this is a definition of humility. And it is humility we need most, as well as proficiency and competency, when we are dealing with the brokenness of others. I ended my speech with a story about a missionary friend, unjustly imprisoned, for whom I had undergone an intense experience of prayer, only to discover he had been released two weeks before my nighttime vigil. Then I talked about the fact that this was not necessarily disheartening; instead, it taught me that our prayers (and our efforts) are applied to the world's needs in ways we cannot possibly understand but must simply accept.

Several weeks after the convention I received a letter from a psychologist who had been at the banquet. He writes of his intellectual posture during my speech:

> I began in my analytic fashion to pick apart your "non-speech." But my normally cynical and ruthless attempts to wring something trite or "overspiritualized" from a speaker's words were melted. I respectfully acknowledged your

> vulnerability and settled into allowing you to minister from your soul to mine. This was a curious thing for you to have disengaged my professionally disciplined observing ego. As a colleague and I drove home on Sunday, we listened again to you on tape. . . . I am left with a sense of wholeness as if I were your friend in prison and that you had come close to me in your prayers.

Here was a speech I had ripped to pieces and rearranged while sitting at the speakers' table (all the while, carrying on polite chitchat over the roast beef), delivered to a group that had virtually nothing to learn from me professionally, and given at the end of a long weekend when everyone, certainly, was benumbed with information overload. And still, this man had felt held, "as if I were your friend in prison and that you had come close to me in your prayers." How remarkable. How humbling.

Now the funniest part of this incident was that I didn't understand most of the psychological jargon this kind man used in his letter (which I have not included here) to evaluate my communication "techniques." I had to track down a close friend who holds a Ph.D. in clinical counseling and beg her to interpret the language. It was an excellent example of the very truth I was teaching: We are not nearly as important as we think we are, but we are much more important than we know.

We are always learning about ourselves and we will make mistakes in holding. I may never fully understand the frantic clawing (or misbehavior) of that one tormented by fear. But I can learn to say, "This is what has happened to you; you have been waylaid. You are the victim of a drive-by emotional shooting. You are here in this place, it is called depression, it is called sorrow. I am beside you. I will not leave you to suffer alone. You do not need to be afraid. Fear will only abrade the pain. I cannot keep you from entering into death: you will experience the divorce, the business failure, the crippling disorder. Despite all my efforts, you will enter that dark place. But I can hold your hand. I can sit by your bedside. I can ease your journey. I can make sure you still hear the sound of my voice."

Over the past thirty-five years, I have done many things poorly in terms of people care. I have been neglectful when I should have been active. I have fled from the blood and gore, from the mess of others' distresses. But I have learned a few profound truths. Perhaps you know them already. Take what you can learn from my journey; discard what is not needful.

We are always learners in this business of life, and the parameters of mercy and its depths will lead us into the limitless academics of charity. And we will make mistakes along the way (but we can learn from them).

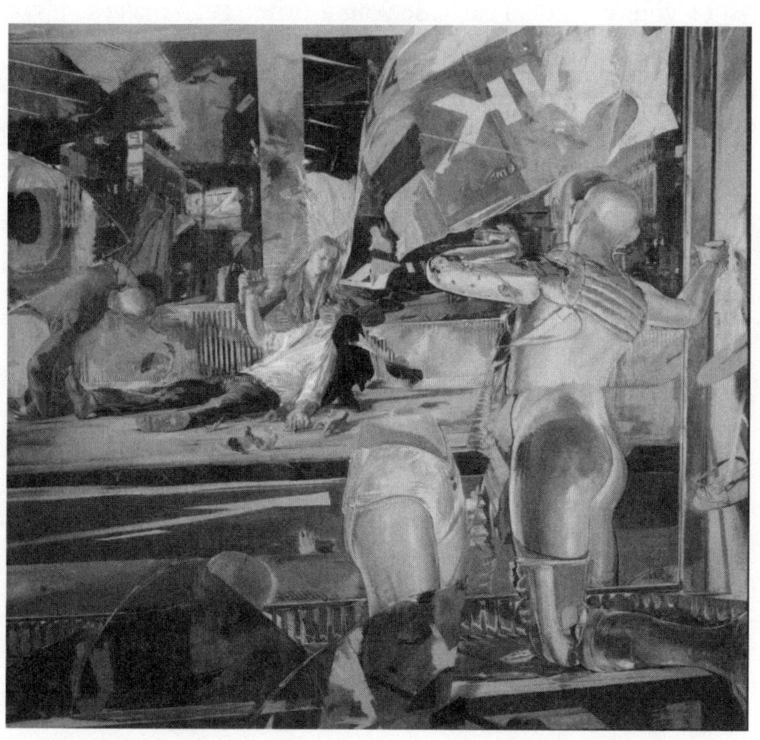

The act of holding another person requires the comforter to abandon all pride and concern for what others think. This painting depicts such a pietà moment as the woman, surrounded by unfeeling masses, stops to care. *Jerome Paul Witkin,* Kill Joy: To the Passions of Käthe Kollwitz, *1975-76, Oil on canvas, Palmer Museum of Art, The Pennsylvania State University, 76.47*

Chapter Six

Other Lessons on Comforting One Another

One of the women in my Covenant Group, Linda Richardson, shared this story of an acquaintance, Jeanie. Jeanie had an adopted brother, Donald. Like his adopted father, Donald became an alcoholic, starting to drink at a very young age and continuing for his whole adult life. A brief, unhappy marriage ended in his twenties, and as long as Jeanie's mother lived, there was a history of financial bailouts.

The mother died from Alzheimer's disease in 1981, after which Jeanie stepped into the role of attempting to help her brother. Through the years, in order to support Donald, a small inheritance was drained, as well as thousands of extra dollars. Linda talked of listening to her friend's tales of her brother's wasted life, of his drinking, his anger. Once, in a violent temper, he threw a chair across the room at her, raging over her attempts to get him to stop drinking. Donald was also a hypochondriac, run-from one doctor to another and incurring huge medical expenses. Jeanie told these stories amid tears of frustration and despair.

In 1995 Donald was diagnosed with lung cancer, which had metastasized to the brain. He went through the treatments, chemotherapy and radiation, rather courageously, considering his history of bad behavior. Due to violent chemical reactions, he stopped drinking but continued to smoke; he was generally grateful for the almost daily trips Jeanie made into Chicago to visit, care for him, drive him for treatments, and fix meals, all of which continued for months. He was still demanding: calling in the middle of the night, for instance, to ask Jeanie to drive into Chicago to take him to the emergency room. All this time, Jeanie was attempting to hold down a job and adjust to a new marriage, her first at age fifty-two. She slept little, grieved much, and prayed for mercy for her brother and herself.

The third holding lesson is, Sometimes we may have to walk through the sewers of another's life (and yes, we may become soiled as well).

We May Have to Walk Through the Sewers of Another's Life

(And Yes, We May Become Soiled as Well)

Most acts of holding are not heroic. They are the simple gifts of attentiveness and sensitivity. But there will be moments when we will be asked whether we are willing to walk into the depths with another. During those times we will not know whether we are making a Christlike act of self-sacrifice or if, in the eyes of modern psychology, we are giving care in unhealthy ways. We will not really know if we are enmeshed, codependent, manipulating for our own ends or being manipulated. We will wonder how far compassion goes before it actually enables the other in his or her addiction. We will wonder if we are not strong enough to allow the sufferer to experience the negative consequences of his own actions. That sure knowing, unfortunately, comes mostly in the retrospective.

Jeanie's labor of love became continually more difficult. When Donald was released from the hospital three weeks before he died, he had finally agreed to live with Jeanie and her husband, Will. The first weekend, he irrationally left and took a train back into Chicago, accusing Jeanie of attempting to keep him prisoner. They found him in a bar (an old haunt) late that evening. And for several days, he refused to return to their home with them. He had not been eating, but while in the city an old friend gave him a food supplement (some supposed natural cure, predicting miraculous results), which caused severe diarrhea. Because the brain tumor had debilitated the use of one arm, Jeanie cleansed him from the effects of this, a humiliating experience for both, and Donald required attention numerous times daily until the diarrhea subsided.

Hospice came when Donald returned to Jeanie and Will's home, but the couple were required to give him moment-by-moment attention. Once, when my Covenant partner was visiting, Jeanie helped Donald into the bathroom, pulled down his pants, lifted him up when he was finished, rearranged his clothes, kissed him on the head, and said, "I love you." He always answered, "I love you, Sis." Each time she gave him an injection for pain, she would tell him she loved him. The last day of his life, Jeannie gave him an injection at 7:30 in the morning, then, exhausted, fell back into bed for another half hour, without the usual "I love you" ritual. She found Donald dead an hour later.

Linda says that Jeanie often reflects on that last morning, wishing she had said "I love you" one last time. I agree with my friend, a pastor's wife, well-skilled in people comfort, who said, "Jeanie, when you have cared for a man his whole life, even to the point of cleaning him from putrefying diarrhea, he surely knew you loved him. More words were not needed."

Today, Jeanie looks back and recalls the bond she and her brother shared:

> I am no saint. I did for my brother what any sister would do, and while difficult to be sure, it was also a privilege to be there for him. We were so very different, and yet the strong cord of love held us together. Bob was not the "bad" guy. He was a wonderful, loving, caring, generous individual who would have done absolutely anything for me if he had had the means. And perhaps in reality he gave me more than money could buy, unselfish and undeniable love. After our parents were both gone, he came from Chicago every weekend to see me, work in the yard, and do what repairs I had around the house. It is true that I helped to support him, but he was good to me as well—and as I am sure you readily agree, there are some things money cannot buy.[1]

Those who counsel individuals and families trapped by the subtleties of substance abuse would undoubtedly address the issues of codependency that occur in this past scenario. And indeed, I am deeply grateful for those who have taught me about boundary-setting, about where to draw the limits. But I also know that love in difficult circumstances is not so easily delineated. Sometimes it comes very close to what another generation termed saintliness. Such pietàs have long been found in literature.

In his epic classic *Les Miserables,* Victor Hugo tells the story of the agonizing escape of the Christlike hero, Jean Valjean, as he carries the body of a wounded revolutionary, Marius (the love of Valjean's adopted daughter, Cosette), from the embattled barricades on the streets of Paris down into the labyrinths of the sewers.

Hugo describes the fontis, which formed in the sewers, places where the quicksand of the seashore suddenly fluxed into the sinkhole of the underground. He creates a long passage in which he imagines what it would be like to be sucked into the detritus of these filthy waters and die. Then he shifts his narrative to the labor of Jean Valjean, carrying the body of Marius through one of these sloughs, reaching a point where he was too weary to turn back. Going forward might mean certain death for them both. With intense effort, Valjean raises the young man's body and keeps his own head bobbing on the surface. Finally his foot strikes a firm support:

> This fragment of roadway, partly submerged, but solid, was a real incline, and once upon it they were saved. Jean Valjean ascended it, and attained the other side of the slough. Once leaving the water his foot caught against a stone and he fell on his knees. He found that this was just, and remained on them for some time, with his soul absorbed in words addressed to God. He rose, shivering, chilled, bent beneath the dying man he carried, dripping with filth, but with his soul full of strange brightness.[2]

Sometimes, despite the warnings of the psychological communities, we are asked to carry the dying body of another, and when we do, we are apt to become soiled ourselves. It is during these heroic passages that we are often forced to come to terms with the insufficiencies in our own character: pettiness; impatience with another's infirmities; shortness of temper; lack of graciousness; superficial charity; raging selfishness in that one's own needs always come before others. The cesspools we cross when we are called upon to carry the broken and bleeding body are often the ones that bubble up from within. Complaints. Resentments. Lack of gratitude for those who have carried us. Forgetting that we ever needed to be held ourselves.

Sometimes, the Donalds of the world are given to work wholeness in our own lives, more than for us to bring health to them. And if the Jeanies don't carry them, who will? Who will take them into shelter, clean them? Who will say daily, over and over, "I love you"? Who will allow them to form the words, feel the emotion in return: "I love you, Sis." Who will gentle the passage into dying?

Sometimes Christ gives us strength to do the heroic works of mercy in the world. Paul encourages his brothers and sisters in Christ:

> For this reason we also, since the day we heard it, do not cease to pray for you, and to ask that you may be filled with the knowledge of His will in all wisdom and spiritual understanding; that you may walk worthy of the Lord, fully pleasing Him, being fruitful in every good work and increasing in the knowledge of God; strengthened with all might, according to His glorious power, for all patience and longsuffering with joy.[3]

We recognize this to be so each time we plead for a little more wisdom, endurance for just this day, gentleness and humor, to carry the burden that has become so heavy. Like Jean Valjean, we too will rise "shivering, chilled, bent beneath the dying man he carried, dripping with filth, but with his soul full of strange brightness."

Throughout the entire plot of *Les Miserables,* a repeated theme contrasts mercy and judgment. Jean Valjean is an escaped but reformed convict (imprisoned for having stolen bread to ward off starvation). The care and protection of a holy priest has converted him to Christianity and because Valjean has been the recipient of *charis* (grace), he in turn gives it to others. Juxtaposed against this is the figure of the police huntsman, Inspector Javert, an absolute legalist with no concept of forgiveness or compassion.

At the student barricades, Javert is recognized as an infiltrator and is given into the hands of Valjean to assassinate. Consistent with his noble character, Valjean refuses to take the life of his enemy, though Javert has tracked him mercilessly through the years and still has the power to return him to prison. The police inspector is freed. Later, when Valjean climbs up through the sewer after laboring with the inert and heavy body of Marius, Valjean encounters a waiting Javert who, in turn, unaccountably frees him.

This unaccustomed behavior so violates Javert's tightly constructed self-identity that it leads to his own destruction; he commits suicide by jumping from a parapet and drowning in the Seine.

> His situation was indescribable; to owe his life to a malefactor, to accept this debt and repay him; to be, in spite of himself, on the same footing with an escaped convict, and requite one service with another service; to let it be said to him, Be off, and to say in his turn, Be free . . . One thing had astonished him, that Jean Valjean had shown him mercy, and one thing had petrified him, that he, Javert, had shown mercy to Jean Valjean.[4]

Sometimes, the Lord gives us moments when we have to decide whether we are going to descend into the sewers of the lives of those who need to be carried.

The mercy that requires sewer-walks will always offend judgment. By its very nature, it will ask us to shatter cultural morays, will uphold the malodorous before those who wash in perfume, bringing "them" into the tight circles of those who suspect outsiders, challenging the church about its own harsh codes. This kind of mercy is not "nice." But if we pause to listen, it will doggedly teach us truths about ourselves. Sometimes, the Lord gives us moments when we will have to decide whether we are going to descend into the cesspools of the lives of those who need us to carry them.

A friend of mine, an ordained minister, told me the story of a paramedic who came to him in great agony of soul. This woman, an experienced rescue worker, responded to an emergency call on a day she was training a fairly inexperienced partner. The overweight patient was unconscious, not breathing. He had obviously been drinking, was filthy, and it looked as though while vomiting he had inhaled some of the discharge into his lungs. As team leader, the paramedic started taking vital signs and connecting an IV, while assigning her partner to clear the airway passages so she could insert a breathing tube. The novice had difficulty with his assignment; the patient deteriorated quickly and died.

While analyzing the crisis, the experienced paramedic began to question her procedures. Shouldn't she have taken the more difficult task of clearing the air passage? Why, in the face of her partner's inexperience, hadn't she done so? Such examinations can lead us to disturbing truths. The victim was of a different race. Was there hidden racism in her? Was she reluctant to plunge in because of the filth, the odor? Perhaps, if the man had been clean, sober, white, and of another economic class, she would have been more aggressive, and maybe the man would not have died.

Indeed, holding one another is risky business. We may lose our footing, have to inch our way along in the dark. We may be forced to face our own disabilities. We may come to recognize that carrying broken bodies is not such a glamorous act of charity after all. And then there is always the possibility that the one we carry, whose head we hold above the sinkhole, will live—and in such a way that, in time, he or she will even be able to carry others. This too happens.

Mercy does not overlook the sin—oh, no. It does not ignore the degradation. Mercy extends love and forgiveness *despite* the sin and degradation. It chooses to be present with tenderness, to wash the dirt and bless in the name of Christ, to lift the starving body, to visit, to attend, not out of duty, but because love impels it. And it is not, must not, be dutiful. In Paul's list of the supernatural gifts given for ministry he insists, "Having then gifts differing according to the grace that is given to us, let us use them . . . he who shows mercy, with cheerfulness."[5] Joy in the giving of mercy is the anointing balm that heals.

One of the remarkable aspects of holding is the fact that we often receive more than we give, which is the fourth holding lesson.

HOLY EXCHANGES OCCUR IN THE GIVING OF MERCY (AND WE WILL BE HUMBLED BY THEM)

The novels of Charles Williams helped form my musings when I was a young woman laboring with my husband to plant an inner-city church in Chicago. Williams, who was physically disqualified for military service during World War I, began to recognize the fact that the peace and well-being he enjoyed in England were due to the death and dismemberment of young men sacrificed in the trenches in France. People were dying so that others might live. The idea began to take hold in him then and became the center of the thrusting concepts that made up much of his later work.

Tom Howard writes in *The Novels of Charles Williams:*

> It seemed to Williams that here was a principle. Everyone, all the time, owes his life to others. It is not only in war that this is true. We cannot eat breakfast without being nourished by some life that has been laid down. If our breakfast is cereal or toast, then it is the life of grains of wheat that have gone into the ground and died that we might have food. . . . All day long

> I live on this basis: some farmer's labor has produced this wheat, and someone else's has brought it to market, and so on. These in return receive the fruit of my work when I pay for the product.[6]

This principle is true in international commerce just as it is in the village economy. It is also true on personal levels. When we are holding one another, holy exchanges occur. Strengths are given and strengths are received. We lift and are lifted, even as we do the lifting.

No Scripture teaches this concept more clearly than Paul's words to the Corinthians:

> Blessed be the God and Father of our Lord Jesus Christ, the Father of mercies and God of all comfort, who comforts us in all our tribulation, that we may be able to comfort those who are in any trouble, with the comfort with which we ourselves are comforted by God. For as the sufferings of Christ abound in us, so our consolation also abounds through Christ. Now if we are afflicted, it is for your consolation and salvation, which is effective for enduring the same sufferings which we also suffer. Or if we are comforted, it is for your consolation and salvation. And our hope for you is steadfast, because we know that as you are partakers of the sufferings, so also you will partake of the consolation.[7]

Again, in pure distillation, Charles Williams's principle of exchange is, *Everyone, all the time, owes his life to others*. We do not live unto ourselves. Everything, sorrow and joy, is given for the whole community. Often we do not see the cause and effect of the negative and positive actions of our lives, but this does not mean they are nonexistent. When I yield to degradation, when

I let despair become my slave master, it diminishes the total; when I stand firm, when I raise my hands in belief toward the heavens, it lifts the world.

One of the disciplines of the "learning organization," a new concept in the American business community, is *systems thinking,* the ability to see the invisible fabric of interrelated actions. Consultant Peter M. Senge writes in his book *The Fifth Discipline,* "Systems thinking is a conceptual framework . . . to make the full patterns clearer, and to help us see how to change them effectively."[8] We err, in business and in our personal lives, when we see only our little piece of the puzzle and not its place in the whole design.

It is important to understand that the holy exchange that Williams writes about, and the one that Paul is espousing to the Corinthians, transcends individual interactions; it is communal in scope and influence. Ever so infrequently, we are given glimpses into how complex and interwoven this fabric of our common human community can be. Perhaps I see it more frequently than some because, as a person involved in a national media ministry, I often read testimonies from readers or listeners in far-flung places.

While holding the brokenness of others, I am given the gifts of agony and terror and triumph and wonder. I become convinced again, at each embrace, that no matter how long it takes, God works, inevitably and ultimately.

One Holy Exchange

As I have said before, I am mostly the learner in exchanges with those who have desperate need. One woman told of having been raised by foster parents who actually ran a child prostitution ring. We often are dismayed by the dysfunction that occurs in people's lives when we really need to be overwhelmed that they are functional in any way. A psychologist taught me to "do the mathematics." How many times a week did the sexual violations happen? How many weeks in a year? How many years out of a life? I began to learn to wonder that there was any health, any sanity. How frequently I've watched damaged people struggle to make sense out of the degradation, to hang on to hope that God would redeem the days the locusts had eaten. I learned to stand in awe.

While baby-sitting with the little daughter of one of these friends, I took this four-year-old with me to the grocery store. Now this little charmer always enchanted me, and while acting as a grandmother-surrogate, we were working on her "very loud outside voice," which she unfortunately kept using inside. Plunking her into a grocery cart near the front door, I began to spontaneously weave a verbal tale to keep her preoccupied (and quiet). And this literary birthing continued up and down the aisles, through the vegetable section, the bakery and delicatessen, past the fish counter, the refrigerated meats, the cereals, the cleaning supplies, the frozen foods, the cosmetics and toiletries. We ended the creative narrative just as we reached the check out counter.

Reworked, the story actually became "The Girl with the Very Loud Outside Voice," in the third book of my *Tales of the Kingdom Trilogy*.[9] It is a gentle tale of outsiderness, of unappreciated giftedness, and of ostracism by a well-meaning community. It is also a story of finding one's place and about being found by one person who really believes in you. All this the work of one grocery store visit and the inspiration of one noisy little charmer!

Gifts given and gifts received. *Everyone, all the time, owes his life (and her lifework) to others*. Let's bow on our knees in humility.

The woman escaping from the network of satanic entrapment takes shelter in the home of a Christian worker. Her struggles with outsiderness find a creative life in the stories of one of my children's books, which are often used in psychologists' offices to bring healing to others trapped and tortured by horrific pasts. We are part of an exchange, a holy giving and receiving.

This truth is illustrated in two books by Doris Lessing, the best-selling English fiction writer, who actually wrote the novels under a pseudonym as an exercise to test whether her books would achieve the same kind of monetary rewards and favorable reviews she normally received under her own name.

The two novels, *The Diary of a Good Neighbor* and *If the Old Could,* are an ongoing account of a sophisticated, glamorous editor of a slick fashion magazine in London. They are written in the first person under the name of Jana Somers, the pseudonym Lessing chose to use. The fictional Jana is a woman who comes to terms with her own selfish, surface existence and appalling lack of compassion. In the first book, after the deaths of her husband and mother, both from cancer (having been really present for neither during their journey into death, since work had been a convenient excuse for escape), Jana runs into an old crone of a woman (Maudie Fowlers) in a chemist's shop. Most unusually, she begins to care for this aging hag, discovering the bright stubborn spirit beneath the outward slovenliness.

Intrigued by the woman's ramblings about her past, the editor begins to write a historical romance novel from all Maudie's memories, and despite herself, is drawn to think deeply about the plight of others. With every hair in place, expensively dressed in tailored clothes, her manicure impeccable, the fashion editor finds herself incongruously scrubbing floors, bathing the woman's old body, running errands, washing dishes, and cleaning the toilets. She becomes acquainted with the gamut of English social services: Home Help, Good Neighbors, volunteer and professional workers. The novel is a picture of transformation, of a lacquered and competent butterfly's metamorphosis into a caring human being, now all too aware of her own failings and deficiencies.

Near the end of the book, Maudie is taken to Old Hospital, where those poor who are near death are housed. She has fought removal to this place with every inch of her being— "Take me home with you. Please. Take me home with you," she begs of Jana, who visits her every day. "Once," she writes, "I was so afraid of old age, of death, that I refused to let myself see old people in the streets—they did not exist for me. Now, I sit for hours in that ward and watch and marvel and wonder and admire."[10]

So. One soul has begun to grow, to "keep death daily before its eyes."

Angry, grim, filled with pain, Maudie has a litany she repeats and the narrator records:

> As soon as I arrive, it starts: "Lift me up, lift me up." I stand by her, lifting her so she is sitting straight up. But no sooner have I done it and I have sat down, she whispers, "Lift me up, lift me."
>
> I lift her, sit down. Lift her, sit down. Then I stand by her, lifting her so that she is leaning forward, unable to stop herself.

"Maudie, you are already sitting up!" I protest. But: "*Lift me up, lift me up!*"

I do it because at least she feels she is able to exert some influence on this world she is now in, where things are done to her, and she cannot combat them; and because I can hold her and touch her. Though she never says, Hold me, I want to be held: she says, Lift me up, lift me up.[11]

Lift me up. Lift me up. How often we think this without knowing it. Lift me out of this failure my life is becoming. Give me a hand to clasp so I can climb out of the morass. Point me in the right direction and go alongside me until I am more certain in journeying on alone. Show me a better way. Help me. Help me. Lift me up. Lift me up.

"And behold, a woman of Canaan came from that region and cried out to Him, saying, 'Have mercy on me, O Lord, Son of David! My daughter is severely demon-possessed.'"[12]

Have mercy. Lift us up. Lift us up. At some point in time, this is the cry of every human heart. "Microbes are on the rampant. / One I love lies comatose beyond the reach of human voice or pain. / This flesh is invaded by a strange virus. / Your slightest touch can heal, can heal, can heal."[13] These words from a poem written by my mother as she sat in hospital corridors while my father sank into a coma, yielding to the encephalitic brain fever that destroyed his mind.

"And behold, two blind men sitting by the road, when they heard that Jesus was passing by, cried out, saying, 'Have mercy on us, O Lord, Son of David!'"[14]

We cannot see the way. We do not know where we are going. Touch us. Give us sight. Lift us up. Lift us up.

The church and those of us who form its body must learn to hold those who are in the process of death, those who are being torn apart by death, those who are lost in darkness. We must learn to be the mercy-givers. Mercy, O God, mercy. Pietà! Pietà!

"So Jesus had compassion and touched their eyes. And immediately their eyes received sight, and they followed Him."[15]

We do not really believe it as much as we say we do, but it is true: As the light swallows darkness, goodness swallows evil.

When we hold those in their hour of deepest need, we lift them up. Like a bruised and frightened bird cupped in a woman's hand and then lofted into the air for flight. Like the father who lifts his darling child above his head to the sunlight. Like the priest who elevates the host before the congregation. Like the pastor who stretches the offering plate toward heaven, we offer them up to God. When we are held by those who understand the sacramentality of this embrace, we in our turn are offered up to him. And those who witness lifting up are also lifted.

This is all in the nature of mercy. When we lift others, we are lifted as well: This is the holy exchange that keeps us humble.

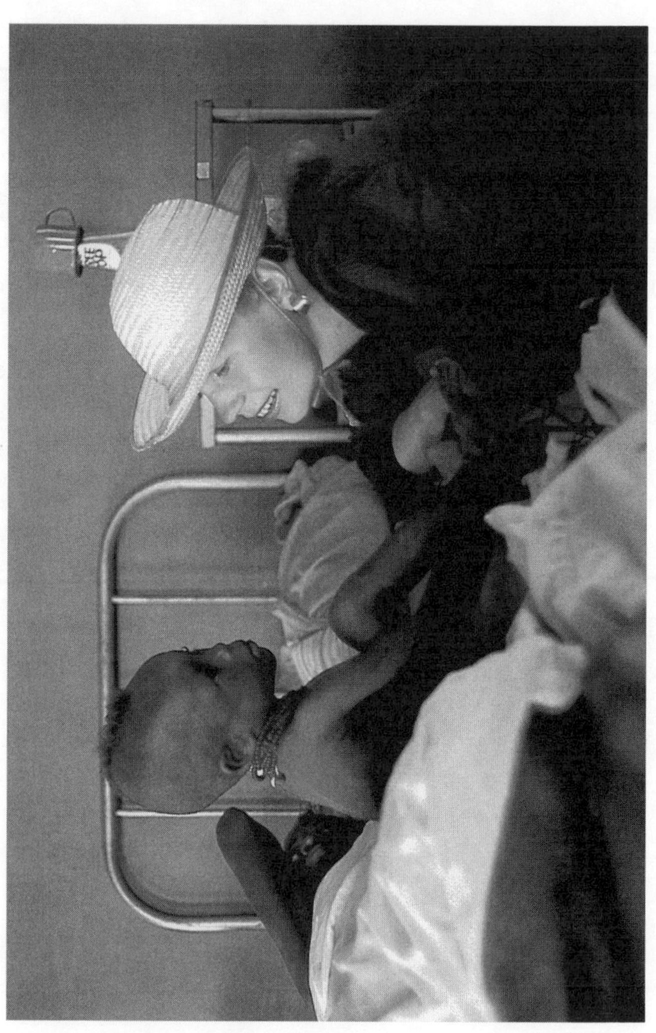

On one of my many journeys through the refugee camps of the world I visit patients recovering from cholera in a local hospital in Kenya. The last holding lesson is that something of Christ can be found in the process.

Chapter Seven

The Last Holding Lesson

I am collecting pietàs. Sneakily, they ambush me. In the movie *Speed*, a popular action film, a bomb saboteur wires a public bus so it will explode when the speedometer drops beneath 50 mph. All the passengers are consequently hostages to his ransom demands.

After a hair-raising ride and near-fatal escape, just when the audience thinks all the riders and the hero and heroine are safe, the saboteur kidnaps the young woman who was substituted for the wounded bus driver, hauls her below ground into a subway train, wires her with explosives, and cuffs her to a pole. The train, with the bomber, the LAPD Special Forces officer, and the heroine on board, hurtles down the underground tracks with the throttle jammed at full-speed ahead.

At the conclusion, the villain is done for, the train has crashed through a temporary building-site tunnel, and the hero and heroine are still alive. Bloodied and shocked, the young woman looks up at her rescuer who has enfolded her in his arms and thrown his body over her as protection. In awed amazement, she says, "You stayed with me!"

David and I have been riding in a hurtling train toward an uncertain terminal. Our enemy has sought to take us hostage, to sabotage our marriage, blast our ministry, destroy our family (six of our children and in-law children work with us). We have refinanced our house to help meet payroll and sold our office buildings to pay down debt to our largest creditor. Undoubtedly, we have crashed, but are alive. Not once in the past years has my husband said, "Why did you write that wretched book?" He has not breathed a word of blame or criticism nor sought to shame me. Though exhausted, we have not argued. It is important to us that as many personal flaws as possible be seared away in this fiery passage. Sheltered beneath his protection, I look up and exclaim, "You stayed with me!"

Pietàs, I am coming to understand, are most profound when formed in living flesh. But unlike those sculpted in stone or painted on canvas, they are fleeting. And in every one, something of Christ may be seen. Look quickly.

This story came to me from a woman who heard me speak about pietàs: "A few years ago my husband's father died three days before Christmas. This meant we had to drive seven hundred miles. As our son's house was halfway, we stopped overnight to stay in their empty home (they had already gone to be with my daughter-in-law's family for the holidays). An elderly pastor, who was watching things for them, lived across the street and came pounding on the door to see who the intruders might be. When I told him our story, this pastor took my husband in his arms and wept with him—grieving with a man he barely knew over a man he never knew at all."

Living pietàs are fleeting. Look quickly.

Another story came from a woman who had undergone breast cancer surgery. "The night before my discharge, a lovely young nurse came into the room. We visited and then she asked me if anyone had removed my dressing and let me see the incision. When I replied no, she asked if I would like to do that before I went home. This, of course, was the very moment I had been dreading. With gentle encouragement, she carefully removed the dressing; I looked down—my left breast was gone. The tears came—and then the sobs.

"That dear young nurse put her forehead right down on mine until I was over the initial shock. How her tender mercy comforted and strengthened me. She had known what was best for me, that I shouldn't face that terrible moment alone.

"She told me before leaving my room that she didn't usually work that floor. There was no doubt in my mind that the Lord had assigned her to be with me through that traumatic experience."

In every pietà, something of Christ may be seen.

Of course our greatest fear is that the exchange that will be required of us is to give everything and receive nothing. Terrible things do happen to righteous people. This truth makes it impossible to speak the glib words, "Everything will turn out all right," because sometimes things don't turn out well; the child dies, the car accident maims, the church splits. There are moments while serving God, often in great trials of our obedience, where it does seem as though he requires this and that, then more, and finally all. Indeed, these last years have been exactly that for me. I have been undergoing an extended period of stripping, of offering up all the cherished things.

Will you give to me your reputation?

Yes, Lord, if it pleases you. I give it up.

Will you give to me your creative plans for these last decades of your life?

Yes, Lord, they indeed may be grandiose and self-serving. I offer them up.

Will you give to me the travel and public speaking?

Yes, Lord, that's not hard, my stamina is not up to the schedule. I gladly give it up.

Will you give to me your material possessions, your home and monies?

Well, there's not much there. But many of your servants before me have voluntarily divested themselves of possessions. Yes, Lord, I give them all up.

Will you work for me without asking for remuneration?

If that is what you require, and I know this does not mean that you will supply me with income. I suspect I will have to learn to do without.

And what about your writing? Perhaps, in the future, I want you to serve me with other gifts. You have been very protective of this area, reserving independence in your professional sphere.

Oh, dear, the writing too? Well, it is very hard work and I apparently am not as good at it as I thought I was. Yes. I give it away. I do find great joy in other kinds of service.

And what about your petty sins, wasting time, lack of discipline in the little things, few asceticisms in your spiritual disciplines?

But Lord. My petty little sins too?

We are afraid of this stripping because we realize that God required it of his own Beloved; how can we expect him to spare us when life has finally readied us for the season of nakedness? How can we prepare ourselves for the work of the midget crosses that conform us to Christ's image? Without a doubt, being stripped is a terrifying process, but we must make ourselves ready to stand quiet and, like our Lord, endure.

Corporeal death can be a metaphor (and I am using it as such) through which to view all the little deaths that make up life. Esther de Waal in her book *Seeking God* examines the implication of monastic spirituality for moderns and reminds us that "ultimately, this is nothing more and nothing less than commitment to Christ's call to follow him, whatever that may mean. What is certain is that it will involve dying, and not only death at the end of the journey but the lesser deaths in life, the dying to live, the loss which will bring new growth."[1]

Benedict, in his Rule written centuries ago, recommends that his communicants live in such a way as "to keep death daily before our eyes."[2]

This, of course, is one of the contradictions at the heart of Christian faith: In order to live well, we must prepare ourselves to die well.

Before corporeal decease, we have many little departures, many little leavings, many little deaths; practices for the ultimate letting go. And even that death, the death of the body, is an outward symbol, an eventual act ever before us that informs the work of dying we must do spiritually. Internal spiritual realities parallel external and natural laws. Spring follows winter. The seed must decay in order for the kernel to spring forth. We cannot live spiritually unless we die to self. We cannot take life up unless we yield it up. Nothing significant is gained unless it is accompanied by difficulty and loss.

This crucial cycle with its ebb and flow of death and resurrection is elegantly described by Paul in the book of Romans:

> How shall we who died to sin live any longer in it? Or do you not know that as many of us as were baptized into Christ Jesus were baptized into His death? Therefore we were buried with Him through baptism into death, that just as Christ was raised from the dead by the glory of the Father, even so we also should walk in newness of life . . . present yourselves to God as being alive from the dead.[3]

At each point of death in our human journey, whether it involves the death of self or the losses of material securities or the debilities of disease or the tragedies of accidental disasters or the betrayals of people we trust, there is a stripping away of all the things we clutch as dear: ambitions, pretensions, our sinful ego. Each point of death can become a journey to the cross. And with each visit, we learn more about the cross. We see Christ clearer.

Charles Williams writes that at the Cross, Christ became "the very profoundest Cross to Himself":

> His will in His Father's will had maintained a state of affairs among men of which physical crucifixion was at once a part and a perfect symbol. By that central substitution, which was the thing added by the Cross to the Incarnation, he became everywhere the center of, and everywhere he energized and reaffirmed, all our . . . exchanges. He took what remained, after the Fall, of the torn web of humanity in all times and places, and not so much by a miracle of healing as by a growth within it made it whole.[4]

Through the stripping away of everything, Christ made a holy exchange, and in that act of reconciliation, he holds the world. So when we look at our ultimate fear, the terror that all will be taken from us and nothing given in return, we need also to remember the act of God through his Son. The question then becomes: Are we willing to participate in the sufferings of Christ, in the ways chosen for us, and for the sake of the overwhelming return to others?

As we ponder this profound question, perhaps we will be helped by the story of an eight-year-old boy. The boy's sister, six years old, had leukemia and he was told by his parents that she would probably die unless she received a blood transfusion. As it happened, the brother's blood was a type compatible to hers, so the parents of the two children asked if he would be the blood donor. The transfusion would probably keep the sister alive. He said he would have to think about it overnight.

The next morning the boy told his parents that he was willing to donate blood. At the hospital he was placed on a gurney beside his sister. Hooking up the children to the technical apparatus, the nurse withdrew a pint of blood from the boy, and then began the IV drip, which would give a chance of life to the little girl. The brother rested a long while in silence while the blood flowed into his sister. Finally the doctor came to check on how he was doing.

The little boy looked up and asked, "How soon will it be until I start to die?"

Are we willing to die like the child? We must remember the purpose in all these painful strippings away. Paul, who knew everything about all the little deaths, wrote, "Blessed be the God and Father of our Lord Jesus Christ, the Father of mercies and

God of all comfort, who comforts us in all our tribulation, that we may be able to comfort those who are in any trouble, with the comfort with which we ourselves are comforted by God."[5] Our pain, like Christ's, can bring healing to others.

Are we willing to be stripped naked before God? Can we yield ourselves to his puzzling methods? Can we submit to his workings? The theologian Philip Brooks prayed:

> O Lord, by all Your dealings with us, whether of joy or pain, of light or darkness, let us be brought to You. Let us value no treatment of Your grace simply because it makes us happy or because it makes us sad, because it gives us or denies us what we want; but may all that You send us bring us to You, that knowing Your perfectness, we may be sure in every disappointment that You are still enlightening us, and in every enforced idleness that You are still using us; yes, in every death You are giving us life, as in His death You gave life to Your Son, our Saviour Jesus Christ. Amen.[6]

Do we want to pay the cost to become comforters?

Before we look at the last holding lesson, let us remind ourselves of those lessons we have already learned:

Touch is important. (It can heal.)

We are going to make mistakes. (But we can learn from them.)

We may have to walk through the sewers of another's life. (And yes, we may become soiled as well.)

Holy exchanges occur in the giving of mercy (and we will be humbled by them).

And the fifth and last holding lesson is this: When we hold others in their moments of deepest pain, Christ is always near (but we will have to learn to recognize him in the silence).

CHRIST IS ALWAYS NEAR
(BUT WE WILL HAVE TO LEARN TO RECOGNIZE HIM IN THE SILENCE)

I confess that I have pretensions to be part of the literati, those erudite aficionados who love and interpret the literature of our culture. However, reality has convinced me that my aspirations are exactly that—pretensions. When I am with true intellectuals (as opposed to myself, a bright, but basically ordinary thinker), I find myself gasping for breath as I scramble to keep up, always on the underside of the bubble of brilliance, glimpsing the light casting its prisms on the surface.

A lecture at the Art Institute of Chicago by the internationally renowned Mexican writer Carlos Fuentes convinced me again of how little I know. After reading from a new work to an audience of some three thousand, Fuentes and another writer, a poet, sat on stools on the stage and entered into a conversation.

They vaulted together through world politics, contemporary literature, and the lectures of Nobel prize authors; it was like being on a great refreshing river in which the two men navigated the rapids without mishap, calling out to one another in a variety of languages and answering in kind. I felt like a spectator upon whose face the river had sprayed some spume. My eyes were damp and I could cry out, "Oh, the spray! The spray!" But I had no more business in the mighty river than a nonswimmer does in an abandoned stone quarry pool.

For decades, I have had a similar relationship with the writer Fyodor Dostoyevsky. I reread his canon and consider him one of the great literary artists and Christian prophets of the last century. I plunge my bare toe into the vast surface of his writings, and every so often I wade knee-deep, but soon rush to the shore again, due to the limits of my own mental capacities.

One essential understanding to the reading of Dostoyevsky is that he is consummately, passionately Christian, a central meaning secular critics often miss in their analysis of his works. George A. Panichas, in his book *The Burden of Vision: Dostoyevsky's Spiritual Art*, writes, "Fyodor Dostoyevsky's highest and most permanent achievement as a novelist lies in his exploration of man's religious complex, his world, his fate. . . . Religion is the matrix of Dostoyevsky's sensibility; it is, first and last, the education and discipline of his imagination."[7]

Once this point has been established, that the Dostoyevskian worldview is essentially religious and fundamentally Christian, then I am greatly assisted in my understanding of this brilliant writer. In *The Idiot* Dostoyevsky includes one of the most powerful death vigils in all of literature, giving me the needed picture to portray the truth of this last holding lesson. Many literary analysts claim that Prince Myshkin, the hero of the book, is a Christ figure. I think of the prince, instead, as only *partially* portraying Christlike qualities. The writer gives Myshkin a duality of nature; he is a prince and an epileptic; his princeship a sign of his supernal and exalted self, and the epilepsy a kind of stigma of human frailty.

But the partiality of the Christ figure in this novel is shown by the fact that Myshkin is not a triumphant Christ. He is instead only a sacrificed Christ. The prince represents the terrible power of humility confronting an ego-fanatic culture that is stunned when challenged by this power but cannot yield to it. *The Idiot* is a dialogue in which Myshkin's voice cries out against the voice of the world, and that world is one that continually refuses the offer of grace. Dostoyevsky insists that modern consciousness will attempt to eradicate anything transcendent and not of its own creation. And this is one reason I consider him a prophet for our times.

The prince is to marry Nastasya Filippovna; a union with redemptive meaning. She, a woman of enormous beauty, has been seduced in her early life by the man to whose care she was a ward; her soul now is in deep distress, and she is wooed ardently through the pages by Rogozhin, the sensualist, with whom she is psychologically entangled. The night of the marriage ceremony, standing at the door of the church with the wedding guests waiting, the bride abandons Myshkin (turns her back on redemption), runs off with Rogozhin, who murders her out of passions that have succumbed to the frenzy of madness. The madman places Nastasya's body on a bed in his study, covered with a cloth, a sheet with four uncorked bottles of disinfectant beside her. The curtain between the alcove where the corpse lies and the rest of the room is drawn.

Truly Christlike, Myshkin comes the next day, searching for these two who have betrayed and abandoned him. Finally, around evening Rogozhin returns to his rooms; the men enter together.

"Where is Natasya Filippovna?" the prince whispers.

"There."

Dostoevsky describes this bed of death:

> All around in disorder at the foot of the bed, on chairs beside it, and even on the floor, clothes had been flung in disorder; a rich white silk dress, flowers, and ribbons. . . . At the end of

> the bed there was a crumpled heap of lace and on the white lace the toes of a bare foot peeped out from under the sheet; it seemed as though it had been carved out of marble and it was horridly still.[8]

Here we have not only a description of death, but a violation of the wedding garments. The prince begins to tremble in terror. The murderer has obviously gone mad. Rogozhin makes up a bed for them both in the room (the tomb), saying,

> We'll stay the night here together. There is no bed but that one, and I thought we might take the pillows off the two sofas and make up a bed here for you and me beside the curtain, so that we can be together. For if they come in and begin looking round or searching, they'll see her at once and take her away. They'll begin questioning me, I shall say it was me, and they'll take me away at once. So let her lie here now beside, beside you and me.[9]

So the great artist paints this death vigil with words of horror and unaccountable tenderness. The soft light of early day creeps into the room:

> From time to time Rogozhin began suddenly and incoherently muttering in a loud harsh voice, he began shouting and laughing. Then Myshkin stretched out his trembling hand to him and softly touched his head, his hair, stroking them and stroking his cheeks. . . . Tears flowed from his eyes on to Rogozhin's cheeks, but perhaps he did not notice then his own tears and was quite unaware of them.[10]

In all of literature there is no more profound picture of Christ-like lamentation. Christ came to redeem the lost. He lies down beside us, the murdered and the murderer, sharing the very bed of our transgression, stroking our hair as we rant and rave and descend into madness because we have refused to accept his offer of spiritual marriage. His tears drop upon our cheeks.

Though there is one last chapter, a denouement, it is with this scene that Dostoyevsky really ends *The Idiot*. Humankind has refused "so great a salvation" and is trapped in the despair of a Good Friday without end:

> After many hours the doors were opened and people came in, they found the murderer completely unconscious and raving. Myshkin was sitting beside him motionless on the floor, and every time the delirious man broke into screaming or babble, he hastened to pass his trembling hand softly over his hair and cheeks, as though caressing and soothing him. But by now he could understand no questions he was asked and did not recognize the people surrounding him.[11]

This picture of Christ resting through the night in death's vigil, in the bed of the murderer, beside the slaughtered body of the loved one, has helped me during my own time of sorrows. When I could not hear his voice speaking to my soul, or know his wherefores, or understand the whereabouts of divine action, I was assisted in resting patiently in the pain when I thought of Myshkin stroking Rogozhin's face, of the prince's tears dropping on the cheeks of the madman.

The ancient writers spoke of the silence of God, those moments of intense human suffering and need when God does not speak, as *Deus Absconditus*—the God who is hidden. We must learn that God is in the silence.

The God Who Is Hidden

In torturous passages, either of the body, the soul, or the mind, it seems as though the God who we as little children learned was "everywhere present" is, indeed, absent. Not there, not concerned about our being torn and wrenched and trampled.

Most people in the midst of unremitting pain wonder, "Where is God in all this?" or "What is he doing?"

Nothing seems to evoke a divine response. Not bargaining. Not cursing. Not abandoning our cherished dreams. Not sacrifice (I will give up . . . give up . . . give up). The pressure continues and God does not answer.

In truth, God has not abandoned us. We are not forsaken. But for his own purposes, he is now silent.

It is only when we have suffered, when the suffering has seemed unremitting, and when we have finally stopped screaming at God and accepted that it is in this silence that a deep purpose is being worked beyond our knowing— only then we can begin to really understand the final holding lesson: Christ is here. He is just weeping with us, like the friend outside of Lazarus's tomb. Some day. Some day, this Good Friday will end. We will hear his voice calling, "Come forth. Come out. Unbind him. Let him go."

Meanwhile, we will hold that one in deepest need. We will hold him, hold her. Having learned the lessons of silence, we will say little ourselves. Only, Christ have mercy. Lord, have mercy. *Christe eleison. Kyrie eleison.*

Part Two

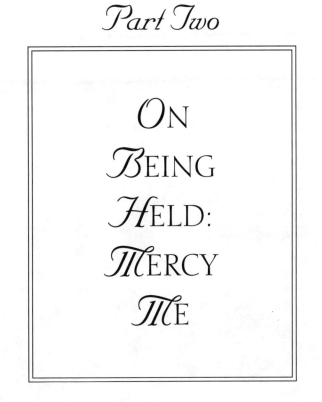

On Being Held: Mercy Me

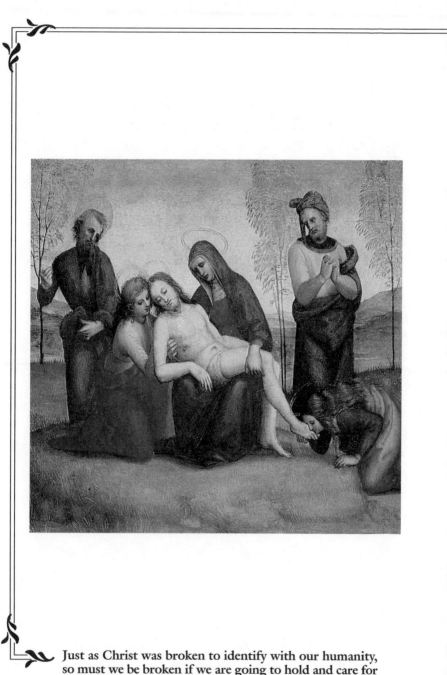

Just as Christ was broken to identify with our humanity, so must we be broken if we are going to hold and care for those suffering around us. *Raphael,* The Pietà, *1483-1520, painting. Photo courtesy of Corbis-Bettmann*

Chapter Eight

Midget Crosses

There is an awkward pietà in Tolstoy's small masterpiece, *The Death of Ivan Ilych*. When my brother-in-law brought this to my attention, the visual image it evoked seemed too odd to be useful. But then I remembered a similar odd discomfort in allowing others to hold me in moments of personal distress. I discovered lessons to be drawn from this account. As Ivan Ilych lies dying, in great physical pain, his servant, Gerasim, elevates Ilych's legs onto his own shoulders to help ease his patient's discomfort. Awkward, ungainly, a pietà image is nevertheless formed.

Gerasim has come to empty the chamber pot in the commode; the necessity of which is a torment to the dying man—"the uncleanliness, the unseemliness, and the smell, and from knowing that another person had to take part in it." Ilych says, "That must be very unpleasant for you. You must forgive me. I am helpless."[1]

Eyes beaming, cheeks rosy, white teeth glistening, Gerasim is a picture of health. "Oh, why, sir, what's a little trouble? It's a case of illness with you, sir."[2] After returning with an emptied and cleansed basin, the servant deftly but gently lifts the sick man in his strong arms, draws up his trousers, and places him on the sofa, where Ilych seems to feel better. Gerasim elevates his legs into place.

"Gerasim, are you busy now?"

"Not at all sir. . . . I've done everything except chop the logs for tomorrow. . . . There's plenty of time."[3]

Ivan Ilych tells Gerasim to sit down and hold his legs, and the two begin to talk, with Ilych every now and then instructing the servant to shift his legs even higher.

And so the ritual commences (not exactly a lap-type lamentation, but close enough). It is the only real comfort the dying Ivan receives.

> After that Ivan Ilych would sometimes call Gerasim and get him to hold his legs on his shoulders, and he liked talking to him. Gerasim did it all easily, willingly, simply, and with a good nature that touched Ivan Ilych. Health, strength, and vitality in other people were offensive to him, but Gerasim's strength and vitality did not mortify but soothed him.[4]

I know how Ivan Ilych felt. Pain humbles us and teaches us how to receive. This is one of the great lessons to be gained from seasons of midget crosses and minor crucifixions.

Midget Crosses

Midget crosses are trials that we cannot seem to avoid: a failing business, an insecurity regarding personal safety due to an unknown future, a worrisome family problem, a hostile associate, a lack of funds to realize our dreams. In some way, these midget crosses immobilize us, yet they are a means by which God captures our attention.

I spent Good Friday and Easter 1994, the year after the publication of *Lonely No More*, mostly in bed. My journal for those days is blank. I remember that my husband and I had dinner with the family and two college students in my daughter and son-in-law's home. I remember that we laughed at the table. Even so, my spirits were descending. My daughter took me by the hand and tucked me into bed in her guest room. She rubbed my back and massaged my feet, pressing ointment into muscles tense with strain. She pulled fresh sheets and a quilt over me.

It was good to be enfolded by her care and concern and to yield myself to tenderness. I translated the ancient pietà prayer in my mind: *My daughter, you have often slept on my lap the sleep of infancy, now I, your mother, sleep on your lap the sleep of death.*

The children's book *Love You Forever* by Robert Munsch traces this exchange of love. The story begins with a mother rocking her baby and singing "I'll love you forever, / I'll like you for always, / As long as I'm living / my baby you'll be."[5]

The nighttime vigil is portrayed through all the stages of the child's growth: the terrible twos when Mom thinks, *This kid is driving me crazy*, the messy grade-school years, the exasperating adolescence, the inevitable departure from home as a young adult. At each stage of life, she creeps into her son's bedroom (so the story goes) and holds him in her arms, rocking and singing.

Toward the end of the book, the grown son receives a call from his elderly mother. She is ill. It is his turn to go to her, take her into his arms, and sing.

The book ends this way:

> When the son came home that night, he stood for a long time at the top of the stairs. Then he went into the room where his very new baby daughter was sleeping. He picked her up and very slowly rocked her back and forth, back and forth, back and forth. And all the while he rocked her he sang: "I'll love you forever, / I'll like you for always, / As long as I'm living / my baby you'll be."[6]

Pain is an ultimate teacher, sorrow its tutor. If we are going to hold those who are broken, we must first learn what it is like to be broken ourselves. Our seasons of midget crosses can help us understand how to be held.

THOSE WHO HOLD

We humans are bent toward lies, whole systems of mental untruths that hinder our journeys into holiness. A. W. Tozer, that insightful twentieth-century prophet, once wrote, "We are all heretics by nature and take to error as instinctively as ducks take to water."[7] John the Apostle addresses this capacity for self-deception: "If we say that we have no sin, we deceive ourselves, and the truth is not in us. . . . He who says he is in the light, and hates his brother, is in darkness until now."[8]

The greatest difficulty with these lies, or false ways of thinking, is that we have accepted them for so long that we do not recognize their influence over us. Midget crosses can force us to face our errors. But we need people beside us when we are pinned to the midget crosses, people who bear our weight on their shoulders so that, comforted somewhat during our time of pain, we might consider what good the pain can do us. Gerasim, the servant, is an intriguing picture of those people who stand beside us when we are facing our own pitiful condition.

Through the years I have discovered that the people who hold us best are often unlikely sources of strength. When our friends disappear and abandonment seems to mock us, then a Gerasim appears, perhaps someone we've never noticed, and he holds a basin of compassionate service to our need. These unusual souls understand what it means to be faithful, and most have little desire for public recognition.

Holders are people who stand beside us even when things are unpleasant; they have a capacity to stay unshaken for the long haul. I am amazed by the faithfulness of five women who came forth during my small season of sorrows. For two years, a week scarcely passed when one of them didn't meet me for breakfast, check to see how I was doing, walk with me, pray with me. I learned well the face of fidelity.

Holders are not afraid to speak the truth. This is illustrated again in Tolstoy's novel: "What tormented Ivan Ilych most was the deception, the lie, which for some reason they all accepted, that he was not dying but was simply ill."[9] And then later: "This falsity around him and within him did more than anything else to poison his last days."[10] It is only Gerasim who stays with him, holding up his legs, sometimes through the night: "Don't you worry, Ivan Ilych. I'll get sleep enough later on."[11] It is only Gerasim who is honest enough to speak the simple truth: "We shall all of us die, so why should I grudge a little trouble?"[12]

Truth simply spoken can be one of the greatest comforts when we are facing death scenarios.

Now I find myself asking, Who are those we can trust to tell us the truth? Who are the people I want in my life when disasters happen? From whom can I draw strength when death comes knocking or when bad news beats me? Whom do I want in my life for this journey into old age? Who has the capacity to stay constant?

I've come to realize that the people who help me the most are the ones who have the questions, not the ones who have the answers.

THOSE WHO ASK QUESTIONS

Often, it's not so much what helpers tell me that changes my thinking as what I reveal about myself to them in response to their queries. In fact, this seems to be a traditional divine pedagogy, for God is a questioner who forces his creatures to confront truth.

Consider the questions that God asks:

God calls to Adam after the disobedience in Eden. "Where are you?"[13] This question is much more than a demand for the fallen man to reveal his hiding place. It forces Adam to reveal his existential sinfulness.

God questions Eve. "What is this you have done?"[14] She is challenged with taking the responsibility for her own choices and behavior. We are not really mature until we become capable of honestly claiming the ill that we ourselves have sent into the world.

He questions Cain. "Why are you angry? And why has your countenance fallen?"[15] A question like that forces me to ask myself what is really triggering my rage. Once I come to the actual source of my anger, I often discover that I'm really angry with myself and that I'm only projecting my anger onto external incidents or other people.

God questions Abram, "Where is Sarah your wife?"[16] This again could have been taken as a question about a physical place. (Sarah was actually hiding in the nether parts of the tent, doubting and giggling at the promises that she, an old woman, would birth an heir.) Yet I think God's question was more an examination of Sarah's position in her faith journey: "Where are you, Sarah? Do you still believe?"

All of God's questions have profound meanings beyond the apparent, and if we listen and respond, they bring us to radicalizing truth.

The Scripture is filled with God's questions. God asks the prophets questions. After his tremendous spiritual victory at Mount Carmel, Elijah flees because of the threats of Queen Jezebel, and God asks, "What are you doing here, Elijah?"[17]

God asks Isaiah, "Whom shall I send, / And who will go for Us?"[18]

Questioning by God goes on and on: "What do you mean?" "How do you say?" "What do you see?"

The teachings of Christ seem to hinge on divine questions as well as on the proclamation of truth:

"Which is easier, to say, 'Your sins are forgiven you,' or to say 'Rise up and walk?'"[19]

"Can you make the friends of the bridegroom fast while the bridegroom is with them?"[20]

"Is it lawful on the sabbath to do good or to do evil?"[21]

"Where is your faith?"[22]

"What is your name?"[23]

"Who touched My clothes?"[24]

"Who do men say that I, the Son of Man, am? . . . Who do you say that I am?"[25]

"What is written in the law? What is your reading of it?"[26]

"Simon . . . do you love me more than these?"[27]

God's questions can shake the soul. "Where is your faith?" "What is your name?" Some may take a lifetime (perhaps an eternity?) to answer—Why am I here? Who am I *really*?

About a decade ago, my brother Craig Burton, an Evangelical Free Church pastor, sat me down for a candid chat.

"You know, Karen," he said, "whenever Mary [his wife] and I are with you, you spend a great deal of time criticizing other Christian leaders. Whole dinner-table conversations are about what's wrong with this big name or that big name. And frankly, we are tired of it. Why are you so critical?"

Well, that was a bitter pill to swallow, especially coming from my ten-year-younger kid brother.

Why was I so critical?

I worked my way through all the self-defenses we so efficiently deploy against truth: Who does he think he is, telling me what's wrong with me? Do I really criticize other Christian leaders? If I do, I criticize them because I'm appalled by the fact that their marriages have fallen apart. I criticize those Christian leaders [catch the particular irony pushing this defense] because they are so critical of other Christian leaders. Et cetera, et cetera, et cetera.

Once the hurt feelings, the embarrassment, the self-justification were out of the way, I finally bumped nose-to-nose against Truth. Truth stared me in the eye—the way it always does—and prodded me for an answer. "Well, isn't your brother right? Don't you criticize other Christian leaders?"

When I thought back to all the conversations I'd conducted with Craig as witness, I realized he was right, though I hated to admit it. My younger brother, the minister, had confronted me with a truthful criticism. I needed to hear him. I needed to let his analysis pin me to this small cross. I needed to understand why I felt I was the sole adjudicator of other Christians' behavior, of their sincerely held theological understandings, of their private lives, of their failings and struggles. I needed to look inside myself and ask why I was so judgmental. Quiet before this mountain of incriminating evidence, I remembered all the times I had criticized when there had also been warning nudges—which I ignored—from the Holy Spirit regarding the way I was using my tongue.

Craig's question set in motion a journey into truth that has brought me to a profound and humbling understanding about the way I use judgment. When I judge others, it is a sure sign that I need first to look into my own soul. My criticism is like the flashing oil light on the dashboard of the Ford Taurus: Something is wrong in the engine.

Christ teaches us self-examination in the Sermon on the Mount when he instructs us to look at the beam in our own eye before we harangue others about motes in their eyes. His questions are a means of forcing that inward consideration. Yet as we all know, and James makes clear, hearing Scripture and doing Scripture are very different postures.[28]

Criticism, of course, can be one of the midget crosses we must bear. Would that all who criticize were loving truth-bearers, kind questioners strong enough to leave their challenges open-ended and unconcluded, servants who trust that God will do his work in his time.

Unfortunately, most critics are as blinded by their own unrecognized spirit of judgment as I have been. Sometimes what critics say has no truth in it; sometimes what they say can lead others away from truth; sometimes what they say holds only a nugget of truth. Nevertheless, when I am the one being criticized, it is my role to listen to their harangue and to take the diatribe before God and ask what it is in the criticism that I need to know.

My errors in the eyes of God, known only to him and to me, are grave indeed. Never have I defamed anyone publicly, at least not intentionally so, but, oh, my dining room table has often been a slaughterhouse! Amy Carmichael, in her little book of meditations titled *If,* writes, "If I feel bitterly towards those who condemn me, as it seems to me, unjustly, forgetting that if they knew me as I know myself they would condemn me much more, then I know nothing of Calvary love."[29]

Christian brothers and sisters, our critics, some harsh and some even vicious, can afford us great opportunities for growth. As Corrie ten Boom once wrote, "Critics are our best unpaid counselors."[30]

- Criticism can force us to find the harmful judgment against others that we have so cavalierly allowed to breed within our souls.
- Criticism can force a painful pause that the Holy Spirit, that divine opportunist, invariably uses to capture our attention and teach us lessons.
- Criticism can become a window through which we observe how Christ would deal with this same difficulty.

- Criticism can help break away the hard husk that surrounds our ego and prevents the growth of the Christ life within us.

The last four chapters of *The Death of Ivan Ilych* are a remarkable chronicle of conversion, albeit a deathbed conversion. First, there is a Job-like struggle with God, "Why hast Thou done all this?"[31] Second, there is a coming to terms with those epiphanic understandings that lead the dying Ivan to see his own spiritual deprivation. "His mental sufferings were due to the fact that that night, as he looked at Gerasim's sleepy, good-natured face with its prominent cheek-bones, the question suddenly occurred to him: "'What if my whole life has really been wrong?'"[32] Last, Ilych asks the kind of ultimate question we all need to ask: "Why are you really doing all the things you are doing?"[33] We desperately need holders who are not afraid to challenge us with truth.

What about the critics who are unjust? The ones who tell lies? Those who are motivated by their own unrecognized distresses?

It is important to understand that lies and unjust criticism must not be internalized. The spoiler, that father of lies, can use those untruths to defile our souls.

"Have I not seen my own error?" I inquire when puzzling criticism comes my way. "Is this true what they say about me, Lord?" *No*, the word comes firmly to the heart. *No. No. No.* Once I have heard that inward word, I must not, dare not, look at the evil accusations over and over; they can debilitate me on my pilgrimage to God.

Instead I can say, "Lord, you know what it is to be executed because of lies. You, the loving Creator of all that is good and beautiful, know what it means to be categorized as being of Satan."

Oswald Chambers, the great devotional writer, advised: "Measure every type of experience by our Lord Himself."[34] Nailed to the midget cross of unjust, even evil, criticism, I can go deeper into my identification with the life, suffering, death, burial, and resurrection of Christ. So even the harsh critic has his or her purpose in God's redemption, which is working its way ever out in me.

Pinned to a midget cross I cry, "Mercy, Lord. Have mercy on me." And he shows me his suffering. Mercy indeed. But first I must cry out, "Help me. Help me." No one knows this better than a small child, like my granddaughter Caitlyn.

"HELP ME"

"Hep me. Hep me." Caitlyn always says this to me when we go to the basement. She points to the framed lithographs and says, "Hep me. Hep me."

The lithographs are student art, the work of a person who attended our church when we pastored in the city. The five black-and-white studies, all different sizes, are admittedly a little rough. Nevertheless, I toted them with me, each scrolled within another, from house to house for twenty years. They reminded me of something I did not want to forget.

Finally, when I had enough money, I took them to the framers and carefully chose mats and edges and decorative inked lines. The five prints, elegantly framed, were hung in the only place in the house where I could hang them in their consecutive, story-telling order—the walls of the stairwell to the basement.

The etchings are of a man huddled in distress, lifting his hands to God, pleading for the Holy Spirit, being embraced by divine power, and finally overcome. Not an easy subject to portray, certainly. Some of my family complain about the roughness of these representations. But the appeal of the huddled human draws me; it expresses my often ragged existence and quite well my need, which I do not want to forget. I back myself three and a half feet against the opposite wall so I can view the sequence.

My granddaughter, with her baby talk, has named them well. "Hep me! Hep me!" she says as we hold hands and trudge down to the toy closet, to the "jump-jump" exercise trampoline, and to the Bible storybook. A child, always needing to be lifted, to be tucked into bed, to be dressed, to be shown the way, understands better than most adults. We must never let "Help me! Help me!" drop from our vocabulary. We need others to hold us to truth. We need God to conform us to his image.

Help me! I cannot find you unless you first seek me. Help me! I will be destroyed by the agonies, my soul gnarled, wretched, hiding its hate. Help me! I cannot be young or hopeful or clean again without you. Help me! I will never be like Christ unless you break me in all the ways I refuse to be broken. Help me! I cannot escape from being tenaciously self-serving. I even complain when you answer my prayers for purity by blasting me with the refiner's fire. Help me! Help me!

In the first chapter of *The Death of Ivan Ilych*, after the funeral, a friend, Peter Ivanovich, hurrying to get off to his card game says to the servant (mostly to make idle chatter), "Well, Gerasim, it's a sad affair, isn't it?"

> "It's God's will. We shall all come to it some day," said Gerasim displaying his teeth—the even, white teeth of a healthy peasant—and, like a man in the thick of urgent work, he briskly opened the front door, called the coachman, helped Peter Ivanovich into the sledge, and sprang back to the porch as if in readiness for what he had to do next.[35]

Tolstoy presents this servant as a man who has accepted the inevitability of death because he knows the meaning of his life and work.

May we all have holders in our life, and may we allow them to come beside us. They are the clear-visioned souls who see the truth, serve while speaking it, care enough to speak it. They are the people who awkwardly lodge our legs on their shoulders to ease the pain while we face the death of some wretchedly diseased part of ourselves.

We need one another desperately. We need God utterly. Let us take up our midget crosses and follow Christ.

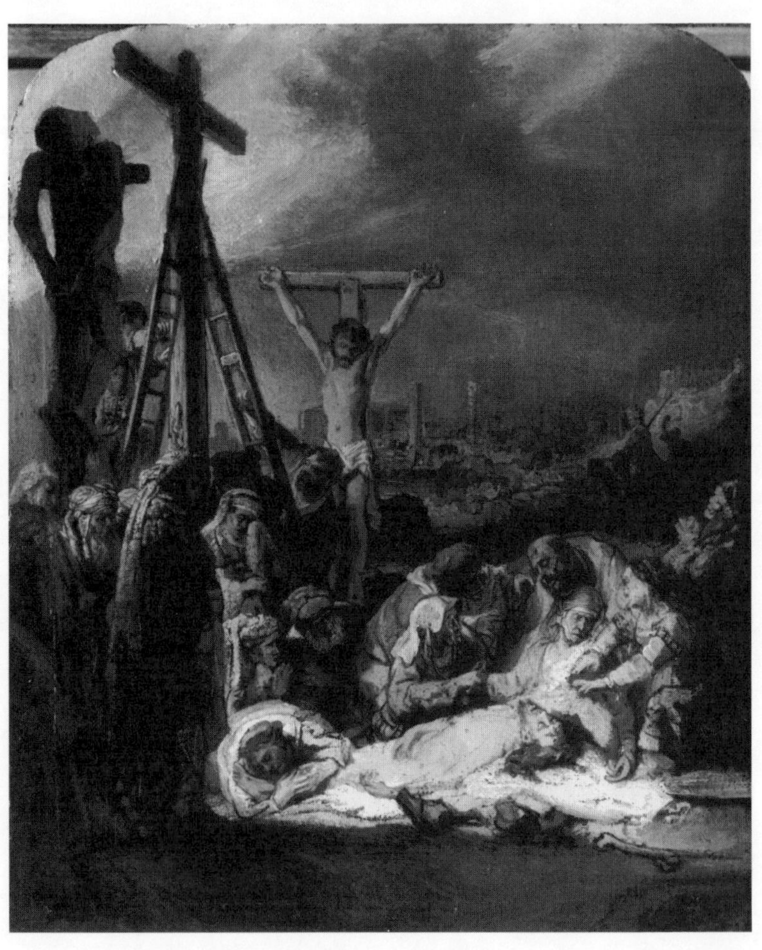

What a defining moment for the people who stood around the cross that day. Crucifixion events in our own lives provide us the opportunity to become holy. *Rembrandt,* The Lamentation of the Dead Christ, *paper on canvas, ca. 1640-42, London, National Gallery*

Chapter Nine

MINOR CRUCIFIXIONS

 December 6, 1994, a year after the publication of *Lonely No More,* it became clear that we would not be able to continue the fifty-some-year-old radio broadcast arm of our ministry. David had been on his way to unite with other Christian leaders who were flying to Orlando in response to the first national invitation of Dr. Bill Bright, director of Campus Crusade, to join for corporate prayer and fasting. Instead, delayed at Midway Airport due to weather, David came home, called our media agency and, in a two-hour phone conversation, set in motion the timeline that would dismantle our broadcasting apparatus. The decision was made to air for the last time at the end of April 1995.

I went to my room early that evening, relieved that the inevitable decision had finally been made and saddened for the cost of this to my husband. Wondering what God was doing through all this in our lives, I was aware of the deep weariness of dealing with almost two years of what appeared to me as unremitting ill. In the time since critics began their fifteen-month campaign against us in 1993, it seemed as though there were whole seasons in which each day brought more bad news. And we were intensely aware that beyond the human critics—and having nothing to do with the human critics—a dark, oppressive force had used this opportunity to come against us. That force was intent on destruction and was intent on tearing us apart and setting us against each other. It had sunk its poison-filled fangs and would not let go. We were facing a minor crucifixion.

Minor crucifixions are those passages in life when we wonder if we will possibly survive. They are minor in comparison to such great tragedies as the holocausts or war. And they are minor in comparison to that ultimate Crucifixion, Christ's death on the cross, in which he took upon himself the sinful calamity of the world and of history. Minor crucifixions, when we are enduring them, do not seem minor at all; they have the potential to make us question every belief we once held dear. But if we will allow it, they can go far in transforming us into the image of Christ.

AN ANOINTING OF PRAYER

The inevitable questions of people whose worlds collapse around them include: How are we to survive? Where are we to go? What are we to do? But more important for David and myself were these questions: Can we choose to trust in God, who promises to be provision for each day's need? Can we choose to believe in God, who proclaims enough guidance for each of life's desperate moments?

Closing the door to my study that December night, I took up my Bible. The pages fell open to a Scripture passage we were using in the 1995 Fifty-Day Spiritual Adventure, our annual program of spiritual growth for churches, small groups, families, and individuals. The theme of that Adventure was, ironically, "Facing Down Your Fears: Finding Courage When Anxiety Grips the Heart." The Scripture was the passage from 2 Chronicles 20, in which all the armies of the Moabites and the Ammonites are arrayed against the people of Judah. "And Jehoshaphat feared, and set himself to seek the LORD, and proclaimed a fast throughout all Judah."[1]

In the midst of this terrible anxiety, the word of God was spoken prophetically:

> "Do not be afraid nor dismayed because of this great multitude, for the battle is not yours, but God's. . . . You will not need to fight in this battle. Position yourselves, stand still and see the salvation of the LORD, who is with you, O Judah and Jerusalem!" Do not fear or be dismayed; tomorrow go out against them, for the LORD is with you.[2]

I went to bed that night greatly comforted but still could not sleep, and when David finally joined me, exhausted, and turned in for slumber, I laid my hands gently on his back, as is my wifely custom, and prayed that strength and fortitude would be poured into his being. My thoughts flew to those Christian leaders praying and fasting in Orlando, many of whom we knew and loved. Suddenly I was convinced that the present and future of our ministry were covered by the prayers of those godly men and women. Though not physically present with them, we were nevertheless party to their great communion. Suddenly, an anointing of prayer rushed into me. I began to shake—and the bed began to shake!

"What are you doing?" David mumbled, a little grumpy about being wakened.

"I'm just praying," I whispered, like a child scolded for misbehavior, making excuses to a demanding parent. "I'm just praying."

"Oh," said my husband, and he went back to sleep.

And then I laughed. I laughed aloud.

On the morning of December 7, after having that clear word from Scripture instructing me not to fear, after having experienced an anointing that I was convinced was enabled by the powerful gathering of praying and fasting Christian leaders in Orlando, I inquired of the Lord: "Is there a further word for me this morning?"

Reading Hebrews 10 in a modern paraphrase, the answer stood plainly on the page: "Don't throw it all away now. . . . You need to stick it out, staying with God's plan so you'll be there for the promised completion."[3] And this is what we have attempted to do. Stick it out.

Though we have struggled mightily in the ensuing months to survive, to manage financial crises, to discern God's plan, and to transition our lives and ministry accordingly, I have never felt again that oppressive darkness pushing in such power against us. Oh, we've been tired, fought discouragement, lost our purpose for short moments, became sometimes confused, and wondered how in the face of God's continuing faithfulness we could be so often faithless. But I knew with utter surety on December 6, 1994, and know so now: We are being held, kept safe from destruction by the intercessions of others, by their spiritual disciplines.

The words *I'm praying for you* have come in a thousand ways—by mail, by E-mail, by telephone, and in person. The suffering in this season of personal sorrow is ours to endure and to learn from, but we have been surrounded, enfolded, embraced, held, undergirded, sustained, sheltered, and loved by this masterpiece that has no canvas, no architecture, no stonework, no orchestration. This living, breathing, attending, faithful body of Christ is a mystical *pietà*.

During that holy season of 1994 in which I was bedridden by emotional pain, I learned that it is at Calvary—with thieves and executioners and inquisitors and the ignorant, with all of them dying, but only the good thief acknowledging it—that I needed to finally, totally acquiesce. I needed to lift my left hand, palm up, as did Mary. Christ could not be formed in me if I did not love my accuser and speak charity toward the one who pointed a finger at me, call the one who cast the first stone "brother," call the one "friend" who shouted jeers when I cried for mercy, and say "sister" to her who pierced my side.

Crucifixion events always provide us with the opportunity to become holy, and we can form the suffering of our personal experiences to the profound meditative traditions of the historic church.

A MEDITATIVE TRADITION

The Catholic Church encourages a form of prayer focused on the Stations of the Cross. Worshipers pause and meditate before each of fourteen depictions. Each station—whether a picture in a church or a sculpture in a garden—portrays a stage of Christ's progression toward Calvary.

Generally these depictions do not move me. Once, however, during a visit to France, Protestant missionary friends took me to a chapel near the town of Chantilly where the stations were rendered in an impressionistic style. The architecture of the chapel, constructed on the grounds of what had once been a Rothschild estate, was so pristine in its design that the simplicity of it all moved me deeply.

Had the good fortune been mine to sit in quiet prayer for several hours in that place, I think my soul would have interpreted the impressionistic meaning of the stations in profound ways.

An Anglican Church prayer is taped to the front binder of my prayer journal, and I find myself referring to it frequently:

> May the Cross of Jesus, the Son of God, which is mightier than all the hosts of Satan, and more glorious than all the angels of heaven, abide with you in your going out and your coming in, by day and night, at morning and at evening, at all times and in all places.
>
> May it protect and defend you from the wrath of evil persons, from the assaults of evil spirits, from foes invisible, from the snares of the devil, from all low passions that beguile the soul and body.
>
> May it guard, protect, and deliver you. Amen.[4]

In an attempt to define what I am learning, I've devised a list that summarizes for me some of the common elements of crucifixion events. In a way it is a meditative "stations of the cross." Reading through this list, again and again, and studying the Crucifixion accounts in the gospel, has become a way for me to keep vigilance over my soul during times of fearful destruction. Exercising a blind sort of faith, I have chosen to trust that eventually something new and remarkable would be rebuilt by God.

At each "station" on my list, I pause to consider Christ's death. This is my litany of learning:

Crucifixion means being betrayed by people who are trusted, being abandoned by those most counted on and loved.

This was what it was like for you, Lord Christ. Help me, like you, to submit to the meaning of this pain.

Crucifixion means being pinioned to pain that lasts long enough to do the work of God only this kind of suffering is able to do.

This was what it was like for you, Lord Christ. Help me, like you, to submit to the meaning of this pain.

Crucifixion means feeling a silence on the part of God that makes it seem as though he is not present, as though, indeed, he has abandoned us.

This was what it was like for you, Lord Christ. Help me, like you, to submit to the meaning of this pain.

Crucifixion means being stripped of all those things we hold dear and from which we gain our identity, being stripped to the point of nakedness.

This was what it was like for you, Lord Christ. Help me, like you, to submit to the meaning of this pain.

Crucifixion means enduring a period of bruising, beating, and battering, to which we bow with our own silence and acceptance.

This was what it was like for you, Lord Christ. Help me, like you, to submit to the meaning of this pain.

Crucifixion means entering into a profound aloneness; people can stand beside us, but they cannot truly experience our suffering.

This was what it was like for you, Lord Christ. Help me, like you, to submit to the meaning of this pain.

Crucifixion means undergoing a gathering of the powers of darkness against us, and in our frailty being unsure of the ultimate outcome.

This was what it was like for you, Lord Christ. Help me, like you, to submit to the meaning of this pain.

By meditations like this, we learn to embrace the broken body of Christ. We learn the meaning of standing beneath the Cross. We become the watchers, like Mary, Jesus' mother; like Nicodemus, the secret disciple; like Joseph of Arimathea; like thousands of individuals portrayed by artists throughout the centuries. In some part of our own suffering hearts, we take his mangled form from the cross. We hold Christ to our weeping and praying selves. The times and sorrows intermingle. Keeping vigil, we begin to embrace this work of God. We accept the pain we would never have chosen because it teaches us more about *his* pain. Somehow, like artists through the centuries who have struggled to capture this awful moment, we take the broken body and with all those before us, we enter into the deposition. In a sense, we are *there* when they crucify our Lord.

During this past seasons of sorrows, I have seriously considered the Cross. This meditation has extended for years now, because the minor crucifixions have continued, one after the other, without seeming end. As wretched as this all has been, as much as I have hated it, I have discovered that it is the Cross itself that *holds us* during the torture and suffering that life devises. We do not really hold it. We only bring our minds, over and over, to the remembrance of it. But it is really ourselves that are held by the reality of Calvary, held steadfast so that our spirits and souls will not be utterly destroyed. We learn to yield willingly to its work in us, and in that yielding and in that work that is beyond our human powers, the image of Christ begins to be formed in our very hearts and minds and souls. God is always calling us to be bearers of that divine feature and form, but this cannot happen until we learn to bow our knees before the pain and bend into it.

And while we are doing this hard work, the Cross holds us steadfast so that our spirits and souls will not be utterly destroyed. God comforts us through whatever torment we must undergo, and others comfort us and enable us to bear the ongoing work of transformation. God calls us to bear the image of Christ.

AN IMAGE OF CHRIST

The pietà that is formed at the end of John Irving's best-selling *A Prayer for Owen Meany* stunned me. It captured my collector's attention and led me into deeper considerations.

A Prayer for Owen Meany ends with the death of its hero in a sacrificial exchange—one life for many. In order to save Vietnamese orphans being shepherded through the Phoenix airport by a group of Catholic sisters, Owen Meany throws himself on a grenade tossed by a deranged racist. After the detonation, one of the nuns lifts his shattered body:

> Another nun kneeled in the bomb litter on the floor; she settled back on her haunches and spread her habit smoothly across her thighs, and the nun who held Owen in her arms rested his head in the lap of the sister who'd thus arranged herself on the floor.[5]

And there the pietà is formed.

The setting of the story is Gravesend, New Hampshire, a New England hamlet with a private school very much like Phillips Exeter Academy (from which Irving himself graduated and gives acknowledgment to his former teacher Frederick Buechner, one of this century's great writers of Christian themes). The narrator, John Wheelwright, is a disciple figure, Meany's closest friend, and the one upon whom the miracle of life and the means of death have the greatest impact. The book opens with this declaration:

> I am doomed to remember a boy with a wrecked voice—not because of his voice, or because he was the smallest person I ever knew, or even because he was the instrument of my mother's death, but because he is the reason I believe in God; I am a Christian because of Owen Meany.[6]

Irving has written a book, which, oddly enough, can be considered part of the genre that is called *lives of the saints*. These biographies (or *hagiographies*) are generally sanctimonious publications that look charitably through the forgetful lens of time and all too often forgivingly eliminate the contradictions and complexities of their subjects' personalities. *A Prayer for Owen Meany* is an outrageous fictional life of a saint in which none of the complexities have been reduced but rather enlarged.

Many authors, when portraying saintly people in fiction, choose a physical deformity to signify the outsider quality that holiness imposes upon those who possess it (or perhaps it is holiness that possesses them). Dostoyevsky assigns epilepsy to Prince Myshkin. How does one portray the paradox of a holy life in unholy times? This is the dilemma of authors throughout every century. (In 1605 Cervantes created Don Quixote, his "holy fool," as an imaginary knight off to do battle with the injustices of the world.) But it is a particularly painful puzzle in this post-modern age, one without a guiding universal moral or Christian consensus.

Owen Meany's deformity—his differentness—is portrayed in his size and in his ruined voice. He is a half-pint child (so small his classmates in Sunday school made a game of passing him over their heads) who grows into a physically diminutive man (so small his mangled body can be lifted to die on the lap of a nun). One reviewer called Meany "a sawed-off Christly caricature, a New Hampshire granite quarrier's son who speaks in capital letters and believes the sacrificial arc of his life has been plotted by God."[7]

The book asks: How does one find God? And then how does one live a responsible life reflecting the goodness this kind of faith in God demands? These also might be the central motivating questions of every devoted Christian's life.

Until *A Prayer for Owen Meany*, literary critics never labeled Irving, the author of *The World According to Garp, The Hotel New Hampshire, The Cider House Rules*, a writer with religious motivations. After the publication of *Owen Meany*, however, a reviewer for *Christian Century* wrote, "Goodness, Irving's book suggests, comes only in obedience to the mysterious presence of God in the world. Irving has hinted at this conviction in his earlier books, but in the figure of Owen Meany he seems to have found a voice that can talk about God."[8] Admittedly, that is a hint I have somehow missed while reading earlier works.

True Christian belief, asserts John Irving, demands a reformation of character and behavior and a moral indignation about the ills of society that is really heroic. As Owen Meany himself explains, "THAT'S WHAT IT MEANS TO BE A SAINT. A SAINT SHOULD BE AN EMBLEM OF IMMORTALITY!"[9] This, of course, is what Christ was, the face of the faceless God, the showing forth of the original intent of the Creator. It is also what God intended for his human creation; man and woman, made in his image, were formed to blaze forth his likeness.

Owen's voice is described as sounding like "murdered mice, coming back to life"[10] and is portrayed in the novel through the artifice of LARGE CAPITAL LETTERS, a somewhat annoying device until one considers that the red-print passages in some Bibles similarly distinguish Christ's words from the rest. The Word did become flesh and force people to listen, if only momentarily, if only to become angry and reject it; when Owen speaks, people have to attend. "FAITH TAKES PRACTICE,"[11] he proclaims to John Wheelwright. We all know this, have heard it many times, but the ruined voice in caps grabs our attention, even as readers.

John Wheelwright, perhaps speaking for the author, declares, "I make no claims to have a life in Christ, or with Christ—and certainly not *for* Christ, which I've heard some zealots claim."[12] Writers like John Irving, who are not working out of my conservative Christian context, nevertheless employ my Christian context (quoted Scripture, lines from old familiar hymns, church settings and clergy, choir anthems, and the holy days of sacred calendars, prep-school chapels, God-words and theology). They jar me into seeing how much, without knowing it, I have created God in my own likeness. This, believe me, is the role of fiction: words on a page that annoy and move us simultaneously; the powerful written image of nuns gathering the broken body of a prophetic oddity, a Christly caricature I have come to view sympathetically, and letting his blood stain their white wimples.

Often disturbed by Irving's portrayal of this incongruous Christ figure, I begin to understand that Tozer is right; I am prone to heresy, following a Christ who does not disturb me, whom I too often make to be the way I want him to be.[13]

How can I be made into Christ's image when I am making him into mine?

Sometime after reading *A Prayer for Owen Meany* (could there possibly be a correlation?—certainly not, it's only fiction after all), I began to pray: *Lord, don't let me wallow in my presumption regarding you any longer. Don't let me dare to create a God in my own image so I can be a comfortable follower. Deliver me from "nice" Christianity. Forgive my smugness in thinking that I know you. Show me who it is you are. Show me, please.*

When a season of sorrows follows soon upon the heels of a prayer like this, we must suspect that God is using the suffering in some iconoclastic design; he is shattering the images we have created about the Father, the Son, and the Holy Spirit; those false idols we have made with our human ideas and that we are now serving. Recognizing this, we must bow our heads, lift the hand in that gesture of compliance and pray, "Do unto us according to your word."

Minor crucifixions are given so that we can be conformed to the image of Christ. In any suffering we will eventually find ourselves at the foot of the cross. But what we see up there may surprise us. The Man hanging on the wood may not be what we have imagined him to be. He may have a different face, a different form, and demand of us more than we ever suspected. In addition, none of us are what we want to imagine ourselves as being; we are all of us half-pints, sawed-off Christly caricatures. We need a new vision of the Cross, which only prolonged suffering can give to us. If we are going to be Christlike figures in the world, we must understand and accept that it is necessary, like Christ, to walk the way of sorrows.

We must not be afraid of minor crucifixions.

Pain, poverty, struggles: These are not conditions foreign to Christians, therefore when we see these conditions in others, we should not shun the people but embrace them . . . as Christ did. *Mary Porterfield,* A Modern Pietà, *oil on canvas, 1994, St. Louis University Hospital*

Chapter Ten

KEEPING VIGIL

"Dead man walking!" the prison guards at San Quentin used to cry whenever a death-row inmate was moved from his cell. "Dead man walking!"

Dead Man Walking is also the title of a disquieting book by Sister Helen Prejean, spiritual adviser to convicted killers, men sentenced to die in the electric chair of Louisiana's Angola State Prison.

"The invitation to become a pen pal to a death-row inmate seemed to fit with my work at St. Thomas," she writes, "a New Orleans housing project of poor, black residents. Not death row, exactly, but close. Death is rampant here—from guns, disease, addiction. Medical care scarcely exists."[1] Her journey into the substratum of death row is a remarkable picture of keeping Christian vigil, of keeping watch over souls twisted by violent crime.

A startling meditation on justice and punishment, life and death, and the meaning of mercy, *Dead Man Walking* shows the dehumanizing effect of crime, not only on the criminals and their families and on the victims and their families, but also upon the guards and the executioners, the politicians and the authorities, and the legal systems that may perpetrate injustices in the name of the law.

"It's not a fluke that 99 percent of death-row inmates are poor," Sister Prejean writes. She quotes Millard Farmer, an Atlanta attorney who defends death-row inmates: "They get the kind of defense they pay for."[2]

Sister Prejean learns that in Louisiana every juvenile who has been executed has been a black whose victim was white and who had an all-white jury. This despite the fact that the majority of violent crimes are perpetrated upon blacks. "The U.S. Supreme Court, after being presented with irrefutable evidence from an extensive study of 2,000 capital cases in Georgia, admitted in *McClesky v. Kempt* (1987) that there exists in capital sentencing 'a discrepancy that appears to correlate with race.'"[3]

Sister Prejean quotes Judge Lois Forer, who in her book *Money and Justice* writes:

> The legal system is divided into two separate and unequal systems of justice: one for the rich, in which the courts take limitless time to examine, ponder, consider, and deliberate over hundreds of thousands of bits of evidence and days of testimony, and hear elaborate endless appeals and write countless learned opinions; the other for the poor, in which hasty guilty pleas and brief hearings are the rule and appeals are the exception.[4]

Without pandering to pathos, this Catholic nun, fulfilling her vocation to work among the poor, takes us into the intimate heart of darkness in a way few journalists or sociologists can. She holds unwaveringly to the Christian parameters of mercy. The illumination shining from the book's pages pins us to the narrative, even when the events she records evoke horror.

As I was reading this work, I drew parallels: The phrase "dead man walking" aptly describes us during those seasons of sorrows when we feel more dead than alive. Emily Dickinson captured this in her familiar stanzas: "After great pain, a formal feeling comes— / the Nerves sit ceremonious, like Tombs— / The stiff heart questions was it He, that bore, / and Yesterday, or Centuries before? . . . This is the Hour of Lead— / Remembered, if outlived, / As Freezing persons, recollect the Snow— / First, Chill—then Stupor—then the letting go—"[5]

As much as we hate them, fiery trials are part of life. Western thinking, due to our technological sophistication and our material comfort, deceives us into thinking that suffering and pain are abnormal conditions. The film *Beyond Rangoon* portrays the plight of an American tourist caught in the government crackdowns in Burma after the student uprisings in 1988. The tourist is a doctor who has abandoned her practice in the States because of the brutal murder of her husband. She says tearfully to the wise university professor who mentors the brave protesters, "I was taught that if you are good enough, if you work hard, you will be rewarded. . . ." He responds, "We are taught that suffering is the one promise life always keeps. So that if happiness comes, we know it is a precious gift which is ours only for a brief time."[6]

Hazard hangs ominous, an imminent spoiler that can shred the frail fabric of our lives. And often, one blow hitchhikes upon another. Terror hijacks our sensibilities and sets off neural alarms, anesthetizing our emotional and physiological systems. We are as dead men walking, our minds and souls stunned by shock and pain.

All of life holds sorrow. We are in great error theologically to assume that we as Christians will not be subject to these seasons of pain. The apostle Peter wrote:

> Beloved, do not think it strange concerning the fiery trial which is to try you, as though some strange thing happened to you; but rejoice to the extent that you partake of Christ's sufferings, that when His glory is revealed, you may also be glad with exceeding joy. . . . Therefore let those who suffer according to the will of God commit their souls to Him in doing good, as to a faithful Creator.[7]

Amy Carmichael commented:

> It seems to be clear beyond question that in the lives of God's beloved there are sometimes periods when the adversary is "given power to overcome." This power need never overwhelm the inner courts of the spirit, but it may press hard on the outworks of being. And so I have been asking that our dearest Lord may have the joy (surely it must be a joy to Him) of saying about each one of us: "I can count on him, on her, on them for *anything*. I can count on them for peace under any disappointment or series of disappointments, under any strain. I can trust them never to set limits, saying, 'Thus far, and no farther.' I can trust them not to offer the reluctant obedience of a doubtful faith, but to be as glad and merry as it is possible."[8]

For the Christian, then, life's distresses are to be viewed as opportunities to prove or to improve one's spiritual maturity.

Pain pushes us to grow, to integrate the intellect of our faith into our daily choices, to interweave it with our attitudes and actions. Suffering is the coliseum in which we so frequently struggle with our titan God, and we indeed find God to be who he claims to be.

Theologies of suffering have been constructed by brilliant and apt thinkers throughout the centuries, and most deal with philosophical questions: Why does suffering exist? Why do the innocent suffer? Why is there pain?

I am more interested in asking, What is required to keep vigilant during seasons of pain? Or, to ask in another way: How do we endure tribulations when it seems that the torture will never end? Perhaps I am asking, How do we hold ourselves while trapped in what seem to be life's death chambers?

KEEPING VIGIL OVER OUR OWN EMOTIONAL HEALTH

The life and work of people such as Sister Helen Prejean remind me that I must first of all be concerned about the soul of the matter. No matter how heinous the crime perpetrated, I must remember that there is still a soul to be tended. In the same way, I must remember to keep the soul in mind when faced with life's severe times. I must take care that my reaction to ruin does not despoil the faith of my children. I tend to the soul of my marriage. I must remember that I am modeling Christian behavior (or the lack of it) to all those who watch me. Christian commitment to obedience demands that I must also be concerned about the soul of my enemy. This vigilance requires a huge effort.

Daniel Goleman, Ph.D., reports on behavioral and brain sciences for the *New York Times*. Through the years I have profited from his articles and writings. His book *Emotional Intelligence: Why It Can Matter More Than IQ* explores and defines this neglected aspect of human ability and maintains that emotional acuity is an important part of our whole intelligence. He gives several guides to emotional intelligence, another window through which to peer as we examine the meaning of keeping vigil over our own souls. One list includes the following domains:

- *Knowing one's emotions*. Self-awareness—recognizing a feeling as it happens—is the keystone of emotional intelligence.
- *Managing emotions*. Handling feelings so they are appropriate is an ability that builds on self-awareness.
- *Motivating oneself*. Marshaling emotions in the service of a goal is essential for paying attention, for self-motivation and mastery, and for creativity.
- *Recognizing emotions in others*. Empathy, another ability that builds on emotional self-awareness, is the fundamental people skill.
- *Handling relationships*. The art of relationships is, in large part, skill in managing the emotions of others.[9]

Goleman points out how important self-awareness is in the dynamic of maturity. "Self-awareness is not an attention that gets carried away by emotions," he writes. "Rather, it is a neutral mode that maintains self-reflectiveness even amidst turbulent emotions. . . . This awareness of emotions is the fundamental emotional competence on which others, such as emotional self-control build."[10] And it is important to distinguish between the immaturity of self-absorption (in which I am stuck in my own needs, plight, and hurt) and the maturity of self-observation (without which I cannot grow a healthy EQ, emotional quotient).

Indeed, most of the time, I have no (or little) control over those exterior terrors that press against me. But I have been given responsibility to maintain integrity over the way I respond to and deal with the terrible circumstances of life.

Scripture frequently calls us to righteous emotional management, and Christians infrequently maintain these standards. All the rules for healthy personal life and for healthy interpersonal life are established within the pages of the Bible. (Not one book in the Holy Canon is without healthy guidelines, and the cumulative impact is immense.) But we must learn to submit to the Bible's imperatives. Most of us pick and choose what we want to notice and fail to grow wise by conforming to that which we neglect to obey.

I must learn to master my own attitudes, responses, and actions.

At the beginning of our personal fiery passage, a board member passed on to us a little booklet by F. Frangipane entitled "Accuser of the Brethren." One quote was of particular comfort:

> There are times in our walk with God when, to increase fruitfulness, the Father prunes us back (John 15). This is a season of preparation, where the Lord's purpose is to lead His servants into new power in ministry. During this time God requires new levels of surrender as well as a fresh crucifixion of the flesh. It is often a time of humiliation and testing, of emptiness and seeming ineffectiveness as God expands our dependency upon Him. It can be a fearful time when our need is exposed in stark visibility.[11]

How good to be reminded that God is only pruning us, not allowing us to be savaged to the root.

Recently, I dragged David to attend a seminar at the Chicago Botanic Garden on pruning trees and shrubs. Some of these organic lessons were applicable to our circumstances. For example: Cut back no more than one-third of the tree; pruning more will put the life of the tree at risk. And another example: Always cut away branches that rub; they can cause bruises that get infected. We thought hard about that class when we were forced by the limitations of our ministry's finances to eventually release almost half of our faithful staff workers.

But Frangipane's booklet presses a greater point: During times of unusual fragility when God is pruning us, it is then that the enemy actively attempts to destroy us:

> Unfortunately, this time of weakness is apparent not only to the man or woman of God; it frequently occurs before the church, and before principalities and powers as well. The fault-finder spirit, and those who have come to think as it thinks, find in their target's vulnerability an opportunity to crush him.
>
> More churches have been destroyed by the Accuser of the Brethren and its fault-finding than by either immorality or misuse of church funds. So prevalent is this influence in our society that, among many, fault-finding has been elevated to the status of a "ministry"![12]

I feel strongly that the role of Christ's people is to provide a protective circle around those who are suffering, whether from their own ill-doing or from circumstances beyond their control. Christ's people can prevent the dark carrion forces from hindering the work of the soul. The greatest of transgressions is for Christ's people to abandon those in trouble.

If I was to keep vigil over my own soul (if I was going to exercise authority over my own developing emotional intelligence), I decided that I needed to maintain mastery over two areas:

- It was important not to give the enemy any opportunity through my own negative attitudes. No one had robbed me of the power of choice to decide how I was going to behave. This took constant vigilance.

- It was important not to give influence over myself to immature Christians who did not comprehend the dynamics of humbling, which is a holy work of God.

Job's comforters will always be eager to give their damaging advice; but to invite Job's comforters into one's intimate society is another matter. I began to exercise wise caution as to who would become my confidants and who I would need to be my spiritual advisers. I was wary of people who were negative; I avoided toxic thinkers. There was no need to add their poison to my own. I excluded those suffering from the blame-and-shame syndrome. I avoided any who employed god-words in superficial sorts of ways (those folk who have "got" all the concepts but who have not integrated spiritual truth and are unintentionally heartless). I excused acquaintances who were themselves psychologically irresponsible. Many smart people are not emotionally intelligent; in hazardous times they are not safe friends.

The next area of vigilance had to do with silence. I learned that when we are facing destructive gales caused by human or spiritual destroyers, the example of Christ remaining mute before his accusers is a powerful paradigm.

THE DISCIPLINE OF SILENCE

During the height of our storms, silence was a Christlike discipline I attempted to achieve. In silence, I could begin to sort out the lessons God needed to teach me. "It is no small matter," wrote Thomas à Kempis, "to keep silence in an evil time." It became clear that it was not my reputation that was important, but Christ's. We forget that we are not about the work of making ourselves look good, but about the work of showing forth the goodness of the kingdom of God and its beautiful King. If the heavenly Father, through the centuries, chooses to allow his own Son's reputation to be tattered (indeed, to be blasphemed), could I really refuse to be joined with him in this suffering?

E. Herman, in her excellent book *Creative Prayer*, tells of an acquaintance:

> The other day I chanced to talk to a strong, plain working woman whose mastery over adverse circumstances was little short of heroic. She had much to say concerning the simple habit of silence. "When I was a little girl, my mother taught me that arnica was good for bruised flesh, and silence was good for a bruised soul; and she made me apply both whenever they were needed. The most formidable enemy of the spiritual life, and the last to be conquered is self-deception; and if there is a better cure for self-deception than silence, it has yet to be discovered."[13]

Silence helped me to hear the voices that shredded away remaining remnants of my self-deception. In silence, I asked myself hard questions: Do I really believe? Do I really believe that God knows what he is about? Do I really believe that he would not ask me to bear anything beyond my ability to bear? Do I really believe the Scriptures that teach me to love my enemies, pray for my persecutors, to repay no one evil for evil? Do I believe the passages that insist we are not to sue other believers? Or that it is dishonorable to the cause of Christ to make no attempt to pay back debts?

In silence, I considered the ultimate questions: Can I cry out, like the ones before me: "Though you slay me, yet will I trust you?" Can I bow my head before God, who might need me to be utterly broken and useless before him? Satan's challenge to God about Job was essentially, "Oh, sure, he trusts you. Look how you've blessed him. But will he worship you if you don't?" The vigil I was keeping over my own soul allowed me to ask myself the same question.

Would I love and follow God if he never again blessed me?

I wanted, oh, how I wanted, to be able to say yes to that terrible conundrum.

A listener wrote:

> Karen, I am so sorry for the "load" Satan spread over and around you and David, trying to bury you in its stench and kill God's garden for you. When I was a child, Mom brought home a load of chicken manure to help our garden! All was killed because it was unseasoned and too strong. The next year, however, was outstanding. The garden had been broken down by time and the working of the spading fork and hoe, and now

the nutrients could be used by the plants to sustain them and not suffocate and burn them.

In my case, one of the blessings of this pruning and cultivating was an increased awareness of a virtue the Lord requires of us: humility.

HUMILITY IN SEASONS OF SORROW

In a meeting of writers in February 1993 (just as the *Lonely No More* controversy was beginning), we were asked to name the thing we desired most. I blurted out (somewhat to my own surprise), "Humility!" Silence allowed me to remember my own declaration and to conclude that if God wanted to use the accusations, even the viciousness of some of my detractors to work humility in me, I needed to surrender to this action. How could I complain about whatever means were used to answer my prayer?

Ironically, none of my critics accused me of pride, and whenever I took their accusations before the Lord, inquiring as to whether there was some sin hidden in me that would match their complaints, the internal answer always seemed to be, *You and I are already working on the area that we both know you need the most. Let the rest go and cease not to be diligent in learning humbleness.*

Interestingly, the word *humility* comes from the Latin root *humus,* which means fertile ground. Late this fall, I found time to dig out the compost bin. In a rash of gardening enthusiasm, I had ordered over six hundred spring bulbs, and I wanted to prepare the beds before planting by mixing in the weathered compost that had been seasoning for several years. This task was complicated by the fact that I had also agreed to baby-sit with our little granddaughter, then age two and a half. I bundled up

Caitlyn against the crisp November day and found her a little battered wheelbarrow and a small gardener's shovel. She and I diligently filled the carts to empty the compost bin.

I am often amazed at the persistence of small children whose interest gets captured by adult projects. My granddaughter stuck with me, working alongside, her little cheeks rosy, her pink mittens smudged with mud.

"Heby," she commented after each shovelful of compost, moving about a cupful of dirt with each heave.

"Yes," I replied, filling my adult-size barrow with my larger shovel (huffing and puffing myself). "It is heavy, Caitlyn, but you are doing such a good job helping your Nina."

The emptying of the compost bin took longer than my commitment to baby-sit, and after several days I had planted the six hundred bulbs, cleared out the weeds in half the kitchen garden, and spread barrows full of deep rich compost on five beds, all the time remembering the little sighs of my granddaughter, "Heby, Nina. Heby." To be sure, hauling compost is heavy work, but the benefits come spring will be well worth the muddy boots, the strained back, the exhausted falling to sleep each evening of the gardening marathon, and the waking with strained muscles.

The bulbs are going to bloom gloriously, nourished by enriched soil, tended by the principles of careful horticulture. My gardening notebook is filled with descriptions, the clipped pictures from the supply catalogues, careful notes from my research, lists of things to tend to at the first hint of warm weather. I've kept the order forms I need on file, and I've referenced instructive magazine articles by month, year, and page numbers in order to garden intelligently in this next season. The truth is that because of previous neglect, I've lost irises, I've lost former tulip plantings;

I've lost alliums. I'm determined that the end results of my gardening efforts will reap maximum benefits from now on.

The work of God in our lives can feel like pretty heavy business, so we have to keep the end result in sight. Creating gardens in the soul demands diligence. We are being made into the image of Christ who descended into our humus. He certainly walked through our garbage heaps.

> Let this mind be in you which was also in Christ Jesus, who, being in the form of God, did not consider it robbery to be equal with God, but made Himself of no reputation, taking the form of a bondservant, and coming in the likeness of men. And being found in appearance as a man, He humbled Himself and became obedient to the point of death, even the death of the cross.[14]

Without doubt, all the writers of Christian wisdom literature refer to a time when we will be allowed to live some way within the crucifixion event. This from a fourteenth-century writer:

> Children, I commend you from the bottom of my heart into the captivity of the Cross of our Lord Jesus Christ; that it may be in you, over you, behind you, lying heavy on you, and yet received by you with free and full acquiescence to the will of God, whatever it may please him to do with you.[15]

Or this, unattributed, from my prayer notebook:

> When God purposes to make us die to self, he always touches that which is the very essence of our life—he adapts our cross to each. Let yourself be humbled; calm and silence under humiliation are a great benefit to the soul.

When a crucifixion event pinions us, we must be vigilant. Extraneous distractions must be abandoned. We must concentrate our attention on collaborating in the work that God is doing in our lives; must remove ourselves from conversations, responsibilities, commitments, and activities that are nonessential. In a sense we watch at the foot of our own minor crucifixion. We must remember that the purpose of our pain is to make us Christ figures in the world. And despite what may seem to be in that agony, the deathwatch reminds us that our minor crucifixion is really a work of love. "There is but one love, and it created as well as re-created us. To be made in God's image is to be made to love Him, and to love Him means life from the dead."[16]

One of the works given to Christians is to keep vigil in the death rows of the world, whether they are those faced personally or by others. We must never forget.

DEATH-ROW VIGILS

What is most compelling to me about Sister Helen Prejean's story (in addition to her moral arguments against capital punishment, which challenge any superficial thinking on this social issue) is her Christian faith, so sublimely pragmatic. At each point of her journey into the harrowing realities surrounding death row, a compassionate ministry is formed: a seminar to train spiritual advisers, consciousness-raising marches against capital punishment, advocacy programs for the victims of crime. At all times, the reader is asked to remember the soul and mind and heart of everyone touched by crime. This story is a powerful glimpse into the dynamics of Christian moral courage, and it moves me deeply because I am so often wanting there. Sister Prejean writes about the final months, days, and moments before Patrick Sonnier's execution. She has volunteered to stay with him to the end, even observing his death in the electric chair.

"Watch, watch with me," pleaded Christ in the Garden. We moderns little understand the implications of this Christly death vigil for our own times. Many theologians maintain that Christ began the work of redemption in Gethsemane. While on his knees, with his disciples sleeping, Jesus submitted to taking into his own soul the sins of the world. He was keeping vigil, watching over the terrible and evil transaction in his own self, but allowing this for the sake of all he loved, the whole world. Prejean gives us a picture of what it means to keep watch over the souls of those who commit heinous crime and to enter into their suffering.

Would that the church universal knew this profound compassion. Please, Lord, teach me.

In Sister Prejean's book, the prayer service begins.

> An audiotaped hymn is played, "If you cross the barren desert you shall not die of thirst . . . / Be not afraid, I go before you always . . . / if you stand before the fires of hell and death is at your side . . . / Be not afraid, I go before you always."
>
> The harmony of the young Jesuits is sweet and close, a song that promises strength for difficult journeys. Pat's head is lowered, his ear cocked close to the metal door, intent on every word.
>
> I picture the words of the song echoing from room to room within the death house, the words filling the place where the witnesses will sit and where the executioner will stand. I picture the tender, merciful God-words, traveling across the hundred feet of tiled floor to the electric chair. I picture the words bouncing off the oak wood of the chair and wrapping them-

selves round it: Be not afraid. The words will not stop the death that is about to take place, but the words may breathe courage and dignity into the one who must walk to the chair and sit in it.

The old priest says prayers in Latin and takes the Communion wafer from the container and places it on Pat's tongue, then into my outstretched hand.

"The Body of Christ," he says.

"Amen."

Yes, in this place I believe that you are here, O Christ. You who sweat blood and who prayed "aloud and in silent tears" for your Father to remove your own cup of suffering. This man about to die is not innocent, but he is human, and that is enough to draw you here.[17]

It is true. Scripture teaches that Christ gave himself for all sinners. Christ, we were taught in Sunday school, gave himself for the worst of sinners. And the apostle Paul declared in personal testimony, "Of whom I am chief."[18]

None of us deserve a stay of execution. All of us are guilty. This is basic orthodoxy. But the concepts of divine mercy, of redemption, and of pardon are so mind-boggling that Christ followers stutter, spit, and stammer over their awe-filling incongruity. We rarely see this truth in such a way that our culture understands its meaning.

We must learn to keep vigil.

"Have any last words, Sonnier?" the warden asks. This question is asked in the room of execution, before the convicted killer is strapped into the chair.

"'Yes, sir, I do,' Pat says, and he looks at the two fathers of his victims, but addresses his words to only one of them. 'Mr.

> LeBlanc, I don't want to leave this world with any hatred in my heart. I want to ask your forgiveness for what me and Eddie done.'"[19]

Forgiveness is an important part of tending one's own soul.

THE MIRACLE OF FORGIVENESS

On the Oprah Winfrey show, I caught the interview with Sister Helen Prejean and Susan Sarandon, the actress who played the nun in the film and won the Academy Award for best actress. "We had difficulty finding backers to finance the film," Sarandon reported.

Before cutting to a commercial break, Oprah plugged the next segment of the show: an interview with a mother who had found it in her heart to request clemency in the sentencing of the murderer of her seven-year-old daughter. "Don't go away," the hostess teased.

A picture of a beautiful child flashed on the television screen.

"Well," said Oprah Winfrey, "Marietta Jaeger's seven-year-old daughter, Susie, was brutally murdered, but somehow Marietta was able to forgive the man who committed that heinous crime and encouraged the prosecutors not to ask for the death penalty in that case. What made you do that?"

Marietta Jaeger was forthrightly Christian. She responded:

> By the time that I came to the end of that whole time period, which was about fifteen months before we knew what had happened to my little girl, I had really come to have a whole different understanding of what justice is for me as a Christian. And that justice did not mean punishment, but meant restoration. And that was what I'd hoped would happen with this

> young man. Not that I felt he should be excused; I mean, forgiveness doesn't mean condoning what someone has done or forgetting, as you hear the term—"forgive and forget." Nor does it mean relieving the person of responsibility. But it simply means letting go of the hate. And I'd reached a point where I really felt concern for this young man, who was a very, very sick young man. And I felt to kill anyone in my little girl's name would be to violate and profane the goodness and sweetness and beauty of who she was.[20]

The woman went on to tell how she had requested the prosecutor to ask for mandatory life imprisonment with no chance of parole but with psychiatric help. And how only then did the murderer confess his crime and his murder of four others.

Oprah looked in amazement at the audience, and the mother continued:

> Well, I would simply say that one of the things that helped me to move my heart from fury to forgiveness was to keep reminding myself [and Susan/Helen in the movie says it very succinctly: "It's hard work"—it is hard work, and a lot of discipline]. But it was to remind myself over and over and over again that, however I felt about this man, that in God's eyes he was just as precious as my little girl. That's the kind of God I believe in, a God who's crazy about all of us and a God who doesn't want terrible things to happen to any of us.[21]

Sometimes the holding we receive is one that strengthens us to do the work of forgiveness. A prayer partner I have never met face-to-face but know only through letter or fax, challenged me to learn from the mistakes and distresses of this past season of sorrows. On December 21, 1994, Sam Winslow wrote and asked me to find a way to embrace those friends who turned their backs on me when I was hurting:

> Others, who did not show themselves quite so worthy, will need you to re-encourage them in the Lord. The reliable witness of the Holy Spirit will most surely guide you in your response to these people whose armor in the Lord, up to now, is a bit incomplete. The pain, their self-judgment will need your loving and gracious touch to accept the forgiveness and healing (for them) that you will bring to their attention.
>
> I had a longtime friend in a similar situation years and years ago. He avoided me like the plague. Sometime later I came into a machine shop office. The man's back was to me and he was taking my part in a big controversy into which I had been drawn. He finished defending me, turned to leave, saw me, and we BOTH fell into a big hug.
>
> This friend cried like a child. When stability came, he said, "Oh, Sam! I never knew how difficult it could be to accept the forgiveness that I wanted, needed, and did not deserve because I was wrong."
>
> We are still in touch today, restored and content.[22]

I know that Sam Winslow is prophetic in this word of gentle encouragement to me; he is holding me to accountability. Over and over my mind has been drawn to his letter. (I tucked it away on a wardrobe shelf, thinking, *I must not throw this away or forget where I have stored it*. And I have only just now brought it out from the hiding place.) I must find the way to hold those who have turned their back to me when I most needed their love, to make a bridge to those who have secretly delighted at my suffering, to reconcile with those whose silence has been numbing, to find the means to hold conversation.

This is a lesson for me in holding. I am just not quite ready. I'm only now turning my face toward reconciliation. I reread Sam's letter.

O God! Make me willing! Teach me how!

Humus. Shoveling compost is heavy work. Those with our child-size loads cry, "Heby. Heby." We sigh. Those with our back-breaking adult-size loads plead for mercy. But we must keep the end result in mind. By keeping vigilance over our own souls, the seasons of sorrows will cease, the thaws will break up the hard earth, and the ice will melt. We no longer will be like a dead man walking. And what flowers forth, come spring, can stun the church and a watching world.

Part Three

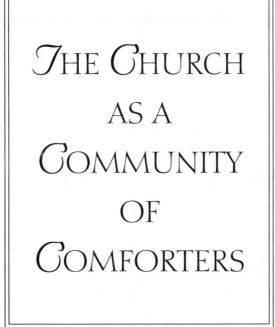

The Church as a Community of Comforters

The Nuns of Vorkuta Prison

Mark Rozema

In Vorkuta, there are nuns who lie face down
in the shape of the cross, weeping and praying
for the world. They pray and then wait, still
as light, for Christ to meet them as an image
meets itself on glass, shatters the glass,
and is one thing.

The nuns were told to make bricks
but they refused. They were put in straight jackets
and the jackets were soaked to make them shrink.
Still, the nuns would not make bricks.
So they were put on a hill to freeze
in the Siberian wind.

Crystals of frost, like knives,
laced tree limbs as the sun rose
over Vorkuta. The nuns were standing
on the hilltop, simple and mysterious,
transforming the feeble arctic dawn
into a rich and burning light.
The guards would not touch them.
Prisoners crowded around, to share
their warmth. And now the nuns are not told
to make bricks. They are left alone
to lie face down in the shape of the cross,
weeping and praying for the world.

Chapter Eleven

"I Shall Die, but That Is All That I Shall Do for Death"

One snowy, icy Wednesday evening in January 1993, I received a call from my son-in-law, Doug Timberlake. By an act of Providence, Doug and another person had left TV 38, the Chicago Christian station, only a little while after David. On the expressway home, Doug spotted David's car pulled to the side, and found his stunned father-in-law sitting still at the wheel.

Phoning from the emergency room at Loyola Hospital in Maywood, Doug reported: A car ahead of David's had changed lanes without warning, cutting in front of a paneled truck and veering toward an exit. The driver of the truck braked suddenly. David hit the truck at approximately forty to fifty miles per hour.

Doug's passenger, a staff member, had been able to drive Doug's car to the office in Wheaton, which had allowed Doug to get behind the wheel of David's Honda and follow the emergency vehicle to the hospital.

Doug didn't know if there was any internal damage, didn't know whether David had gone to sleep, blanked, had a heart attack, or a minor stroke. Could I come right away?

"How does he seem?" I asked.

"He was wearing his seat belt. And he seems okay now but is really sore. There was no blood, and nothing seems to be broken. They're running tests. But when I got to the scene of the accident, I don't think he knew what had happened or who he was, actually. He was in shock. He couldn't answer the policeman's questions. Good thing I came along. The driver of the truck he hit actually got out of his cab in the middle of traffic and pushed the Honda over to the side of the expressway out of the line of traffic."

The accident had occurred on a typical rainy, slushy, icing January evening, about 5:30. The drive from the suburbs would take me forty-five minutes to an hour. The local news warned of hazardous driving conditions. Helicopter pilots, monitoring traffic flow, reported that travel times on the Eisenhower Expressway from the post office out to Maywood Avenue were greatly delayed. My night vision under good driving conditions is bad. In addition I knew I was emotionally shaken, so I called a taxi to drop me at the door of the emergency room. Within fifteen minutes, a driver was at the front door. I had time to pray and compose myself in the backseat without needing to navigate treacherous roadways by myself, half blind, all the while coping with intense worry.

The steering wheel had impacted David's sternum, and the seat belt had tightened like a vise against his rib cage, the belt marking his side. My husband seemed to be all in one piece with nothing but bruises. In moments like those, counting one's blessings is an overwhelming response.

Thank goodness that my son-in-law had driven past when he had and that he had been able to pull over. Thank goodness for the presence of mind and the courage of the truck driver to move the Honda out of the line of traffic. Thank goodness that the car was basically undamaged and that it could be driven to the hospital and that Doug and I could drive it home. Thank goodness that the rear panel on the truck had prohibited the Honda with its slanting front end from slipping under the wheels of the higher vehicle. Thank goodness that another television staff person, riding as passenger, could drive Doug's car to the office in Wheaton. Thank goodness that there was no sign of stroke or internal injuries. My husband had survived a near-fatal accident relatively unscathed. And finally, thank goodness that David's brother, an orthopedic surgeon, "happened" to be teaching at Loyola on the next morning, Thursday, and could check the medical charts to all of our satisfaction and even bring David home after the one-night hospitalization required for observation.

We were planning to leave early Saturday morning for a long weekend vacation in California to stay with friends. It had been one of those winters. The new furnace was acting crazed—stalling, breaking down, being repaired, collapsing again and again and again. It had broken so many times that the electrician, a friend from high school, kept a key to our house. Our small staff was mounting a daily national radio broadcast as well as launching a daily television show. Everyone was exhausted. One of the women who lived with us had survived a major automobile accident herself and had sustained cracked ribs, a broken collarbone, and a collapsed lung. After her week of hospitalization, I had spent hours driving her to and from her doctor's appointments. The home of our children in Kentucky had been vandalized and robbed.

I suddenly realized that I would have to drive our friend's loaned car on this vacation and that my driver's license would expire that Sunday. I rushed out Friday morning to take my test, leaving my husband alone, sore and stiff and bruised. Twenty minutes after leaving the Illinois State Bureau, hurrying home along a highway I had never driven before, I was stopped for speeding and given my first moving violation in over thirty years.

Feeling that we really needed to get away from it all and with the doctor's approval, I eased my very sore husband into his airplane seat early Saturday morning, flew to California, tucked him carefully into our host's waiting car, and gently put him to bed. I woke the next morning, grateful to be beside him in that beautiful quiet place, with friends who cared about us. It was my birthday weekend, and it occurred to me with shattering clarity that I could have been making funeral plans and grieving instead of sitting awake beside my husband who was sleeping deeply, recovering from injury and overwork and the general stress of our overburdened living.

Since we would not be going to church, I flipped on the television in our room, muting the volume, crowding close to the screen in order to hear. Charles Kuralt (I think it was he) on the *Sunday Morning* show, was interviewing Maya Angelou regarding her poem for the first-term Clinton presidential inauguration.

"Do you think much about the inaugural poem?" asked the interviewer.

"Oh, yes," she answered. "I think about it every minute, night and day. I have almost thought of nothing else. I particularly think about those poor seventh graders whose teachers will expect them to study and memorize it."

Laughing at this refreshing lack of ostentation, I drew even nearer to hear the rest of the interview.

"How do you reconcile your activism with your writing?" asked the questioner. Angelou closed her eyes, was silent for a moment, then replied, "I like to think of my writing as my activism."

Then she referred to a poem by Edna St. Vincent Millay, whom she called "that frail woman." The poem was "Conscientious Objector," and before the national television audience, Angelou quoted it by memory. (I have since committed the poem to memory myself):

I shall die, but that is all that I shall do for Death.

I hear him leading his horse out of the stall; I hear the clatter on the barn-floor.
He is in haste; he has business in Cuba, business in the Balkans, many calls to make this morning.
But I will not hold the bridle while he cinches the girth.
And he may mount by himself; I will not give him a leg up.

Though he flick my shoulders with his whip, I will not tell him which way the fox ran.
With his hoof on my breast, I will not tell him where the black boy hides in the swamp.
I shall die, but this is all that I shall do for death; I am not on his pay-roll.

> I will not tell him the whereabouts of my friends nor of my enemies either.
> Though he promises me much, I will not map the route to any man's door.[1]

Perhaps it was our own close encounter with death. Perhaps I had steeled myself so much this winter to manage all the catastrophes, large and small, and I was just having an emotional release, but tears streamed down my cheeks. Perhaps. Obviously, Angelou's words had touched a nerve: I too wanted my writing to be my activism. But in retrospect, I understand now, that at the core of everything I am, at the most passionate nub of what I believe, I do not want to give death a leg up.

After the Gulf War in 1991, I was privileged to speak at a retreat for a regional conference of the Church of the Brethren. A mainline Protestant denomination, the Church of the Brethren has since its inception aligned itself doctrinally and practically with pacifism. In fact, it was the church of my father's childhood. Many of my great-aunts and great-uncles were members. Consequently, as a little girl, I listened intently to their expressions of righteous horror regarding violence and war. As a child, I came to understand through these ongoing discussions that true conscientious objectors were people of courage who not only talked about their deep moral convictions but also acted upon them, often at personal cost. At the regional conference, much discussion was given to the dilemma: How could there be a pacifist presence in this violent nation, the population of which approved of the Gulf War by over 80 percent? How could there impart the relevancy of this moral stance to their children?

The formation of my young adult years coincided with the early days of the civil rights movement during the fifties and the sixties. I watched pacifism function as a passive resistance movement. Black men and women faced police clubs and paddy wagons and fire hoses and snarling dogs and angry mobs without responding in violent kind. I witnessed a moral superiority linked to social activism, which has rarely been matched in my lifetime.

And it was during these days, while listening to the strident voices of the feminist movement of my generation and while marking the pillage of university campuses by the SDS (Students for a Democratic Society), that I began to conclude that militancy, militancy of any kind, militancy even for a good cause, has the potential to turn the victim into the victimizer. I was ill when Michael Griffin assumed the role of God and executed the abortionist Dr. David Gunn; I was even more horrified that self-proclaimed Christians attempted to justify this act, giving interviews for journalists eager to slap their sensationalist bait into print. "It's a terrible act," they said. "But then Dr. Gunn performed so many murders a day."

My particular understanding of peaceful protest means that I cannot be party to the death drums that beat in my culture. "I shall die, but that is all that I shall do for death." The means and the processes that we choose are as important as the ends. I cannot take a gun and even point it at my enemy, let alone pull the trigger. I cannot shake my fist at the face of my opponent on the other side of the picket line or the bargaining table and call her a fool. I cannot use conflict destructively; I am morally impelled to seek ways to use conflict creatively. Many Christian protest movements lose their moral edge by degenerating into the methodologies of evil. Death is given a leg up.

My work, as a Christian, is the work of reconciliation:

> All things are of God, who has reconciled us to Himself through Jesus Christ, and has given us the ministry of reconciliation, that is, that God was in Christ reconciling the world to Himself, not imputing their trespasses to them, and has committed to us the word of reconciliation.[2]

It is my understanding that the soul of each human involved in conflict is as important as the cause of that conflict. I must love the angry, strident feminist and listen to her outrage as an act of courteous mercy, even if I disagree with her. Mortals must be reconciled to God in order that man can be reconciled to man; I cannot be an agent of reconciliation if I throw swill.

"I shall die, but that is all that I shall do for death."

America sits under the shadow of death. By our choices, we participate in death's cult. We choose death a thousand thousand times when we batter the life out of a child or a spouse or a friend with abusive words or actions. We choose death when we no longer object to it. A steady diet of daily television is enough to inure us to violence. And film, the language of our popular culture created by corrupt and violent minds, violates us with its macabre. We choose death when we are not righteously outraged by the wasted human condition of our inner-city or rural poor or by the overwhelming black demographic of our prison populations. We choose death when we are not incensed with the multitude of living deaths that surround us.

Do not the ancient words of Isaiah describe America?

> Therefore justice is far from us,
> Nor does righteousness overtake us;

> We look for light, but there is darkness!
> For brightness, but we walk in blackness!
> We grope for the wall like the blind,
> And we grope as if we had no eyes;
> We stumble at noonday as at twilight.[3]

In our country, under this shadow, lives are diminished, dehumanized. And we, Christ's people, those who say we follow in his way, we the people of the church, do all kinds of things for death. We grovel; we whine in fear; we cast the first stone; we sing death's dirge; we kowtow to despair; we hate our enemies.

When I was a young woman in my twenties, I was hungry for a depth of spirituality not found in the churches of my background and I was distressed over my own superficiality. I initiated what was to become a lifelong reading of the contemplative writers, that body of Christian literature that exists outside of the religious subset of fundamentalist evangelicalism. The works of Thomas Merton, *Seeds of Contemplation* and *New Seeds of Contemplation*, massaged loose some knotted places in my soul. I first learned from Merton of the "disease called spiritual pride" and that "in humility is our greatest freedom." He wrote that true personal identity can only be discovered when we discover who we are in God. "You and I and all men were made to find our identity in the One Mystical Christ in Whom we all complete one another 'unto perfect man, unto the measure of the age of the fulness of Christ.'"[4]

Merton, a twentieth-century contemplative, now dead, develops a disturbing picture on the effects of hatred, both personally and globally, in one essay, "A Body of Broken Bones." When we give ourselves to hatred, he maintains, we dismember Christ's body:

> His physical Body was crucified by Pilate and the Pharisees: His mystical Body is drawn and quartered from age to age by the devils in the agony of that disunion which is bred and vegetates in our souls prone to selfishness and to sin. All over the face of the earth the avarice and lust of men breed unceasing divisions among them, and the wounds that tear men from union with one another widen and open out into huge wars. Murder, massacres, revolution, hatred, the slaughter and torture of the bodies and souls of men, the destruction of cities by fire, the starvation of millions, the annihilation of populations and finally the cosmic inhumanity of cosmic war: Christ is massacred in His members, torn limb from limb; God is murdered in men.[5]

This is a powerful and constraining construction. When I judge someone out of the buried and unrecognized envy in my own soul, it is as though I break the bones of the body of Christ, as though I pound nails into his flesh, press the circle of thorns upon his head.

Of course, Scripture teaches that:

> We have been sanctified through the offering of the body of Jesus Christ once for all. And every priest stands ministering daily and offering repeatedly the same sacrifices, which can never take away sins. But this Man, after He had offered one sacrifice for sins forever, sat down at the right hand of God.[6]

This theology maintains that Christ died for all, once for all.

But I do not believe that Merton is speaking metaphorically. That is, I don't think Merton means that it is *as though* we break the body of Christ. Rather, I believe that Merton means that *in actuality* we break the spiritual body of Christ. Christ taught in Matthew that despite his one-time sacrificial offering, the measure of the way we treat him is in some way measured by the way that we treat others. Neither do I feel that Christ was speaking metaphorically:

> Depart from Me, you cursed, into the everlasting fire prepared for the devil and his angels: for I was hungry and you gave Me no food; I was thirsty and you gave Me no drink; . . . Assuredly, I say to you, inasmuch as you did not do it to one of the least of these, you did not do it to Me. And these will go away into everlasting punishment, but the righteous into eternal life.[7]

He pronounced to his disciples:

> When the Son of Man comes in His glory, and all the holy angels with Him, then He will sit on the throne of His glory. All the nations will be gathered before Him, and He will separate them one from another, as a shepherd divides his sheep from the goats.[8]

The test here of the work of redemption is not just what we say but how we treat our fellow humans; doing is the guaranty of spiritual actualities; the tree is known by its fruit. I am not, must not be, and cannot be death's lackey if I follow Christ. I will not tell the whereabouts of my friends, or of my enemies either. Though death promises me much, I will not map the route to any man's door.

While sitting before that television set, with my husband sleeping deeply in the room, having by God's great grace and protection recently escaped the clutches of death, I found that I was tired of writing devotional thoughts, tired of the way I allowed fear to mute my convictions. At midlife I needed to come to terms with the peaceful protests I felt called to mount, with the moral resistance to which I felt impelled to give the rest of my life, and with the ways I wanted to picture goodness to the world.

Prophetic metaphors unfold in the commonplace of our living; that profound and quiet incident in January 1993 informed the years of sorrow and travail to follow. I have learned how to pray for mercy. Mercy on us, O Lord. Christ have mercy.

We may die—financially, psychologically—and indeed, that may be part of God's plan for us. The Cross is a matter of dying, after all, and the crucified life is God's means of making us into Christlike figures. In ways that I cannot see, I know that whatever dying takes place is for the purpose of liberation. Indeed, "I shall die, but that is all that I shall do for death." I will not raise my fist and shake it in the face of my Creator. I will not complain that the journey has been too arduous. I will not turn my back on being a Christ follower. Nor will I allow the creative voice God has given to me to be silenced if he wants me to be vocal.

Paul writes so eloquently:

> Therefore it is of faith that it might be according to grace, so that the promise might be sure to all the seed . . . in the presence of Him whom he believed—God, who gives life to the dead and calls those things which do not exist as though they

> did; who, contrary to hope, in hope believed, so that he became the father of many nations.[9]

I am choosing to believe in the God who gives life to the dead and calls into existence the things that do not exist. Death may be leering at me and "I shall die, but that is all that I shall do for death; I am not on his payroll"!

In death, even in death, we must look to life. Holding the broken body, we keep life in mind. The entire church community is called to the holy act of comforting. There is no better way to do this than for the church to become a birthing room.

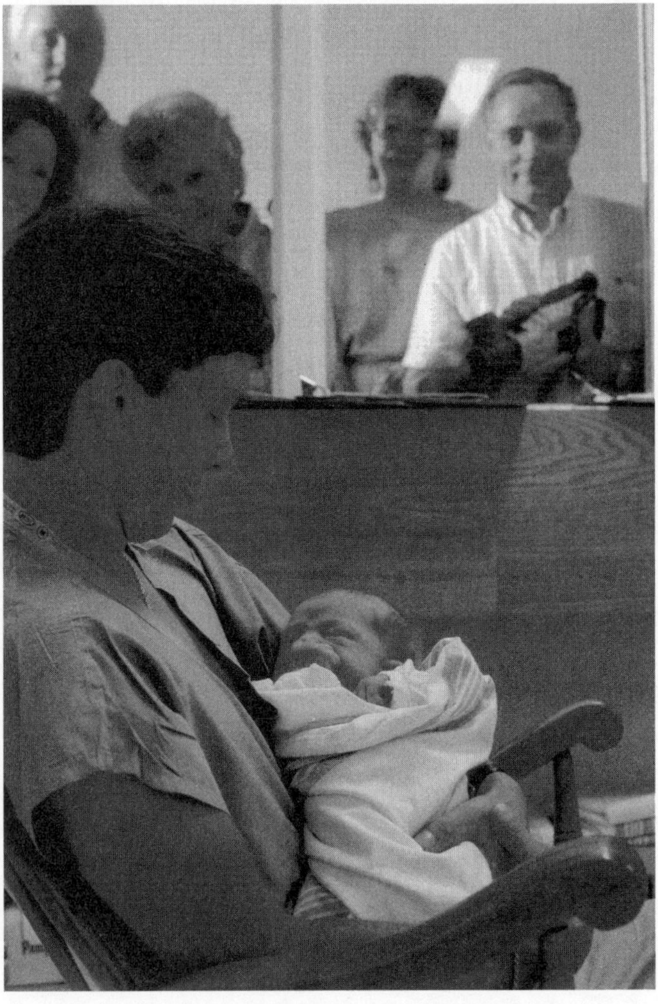

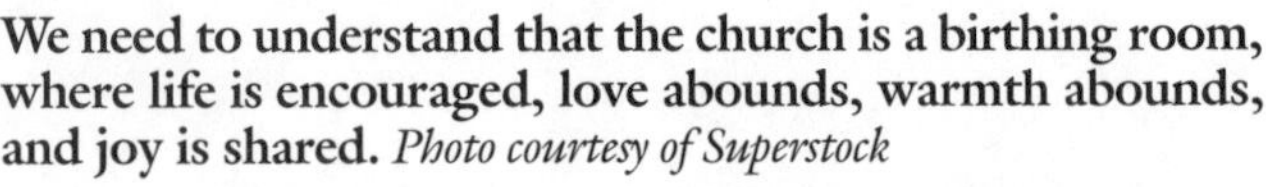

We need to understand that the church is a birthing room, where life is encouraged, love abounds, warmth abounds, and joy is shared. *Photo courtesy of Superstock*

Chapter Twelve

THE CHURCH AS BIRTHING ROOM

The birthing room at Central DuPage Hospital is where expectant mothers and fathers come to have their babies. It's a comfortable place where the labor progresses, where the infant is born, and where parents and child welcome one another in the extraordinary moments immediately following. Here professionals bath, swaddle, and nurture the newborn babe.

At 11:17 on the evening of December 17, 1992, our phone rang. The long-awaited call! Our eldest son, Randall, bore the wondrous news that our first grandbaby had arrived: a little girl. They hadn't weighed her yet, but she was around seven pounds. Carmel, our daughter-in-law, was fine. The baby was fine. They would understand if I was too tired, but if I wanted to, I could come.

Come? I couldn't get off the phone soon enough. The hospital is four minutes away, and by the time the newborn was thirty minutes old, I was in the birthing room, holding her in my arms. I discovered an amazing bundle of life. A head of dark hair beneath the snug, knit nursery cap. What a surprise! My four babies were all blond, bald, and big "Burton babies," my father used to crow proudly. In fact, of all his nine grandbabies only one was brunet.

And the cheeks of that baby! Those fat little bun cheeks. Now that was a Mains characteristic. No argument there. The baby's long delicate fingers. The first yawns. We took pictures and planted kisses on the irresistible skin, sniffing again that unique newborn smell.

We unfolded the thick towels and sneaked peeks at the rest of her body. Sure enough, circles of baby fat were stacked like round blocks up her legs and arms. In the dimly lit room, we three—new mother and new father and new grandmother—surrounded the newborn with our hearts joined in prayer and covenanted before God to love that child, and to raise her faithfully to revere her Maker.

"I will teach you many things," I promised, snuggling my nose into her neck, low beneath her ear. "To begin, I will teach you how to manage all the men in this family—grandpas and daddies and uncles. It's not hard to learn this."

There are quite a lot of men in this family. Of my father's nine grandchildren, only one was a girl, our daughter, Melissa. I had expected her to be exultant over this birth event, but I was not prepared for the exultation of our grown sons, Joel and Jeremy. ("We've had a baby!") My eldest son, the father, my seriously intent architect of systems, delighted me with his tenderness, his preening new father's pride, "Why don't you all come by tonight? We'll just sit around and watch the baby."

Nor was I prepared for my own husband's reaction. I knew he'd be a proud grandpa. But watching him the next morning processing grandfatherhood was intriguing. Oh, yes, he could cancel his schedules. Oh, yes, he could produce that broadcast later in the afternoon. Oh, yes, he could leave the briefcase unopened on the dining room table. It was a little like watching a Mack truck going up hill, suddenly shifting gears, changing directions, and then heading down the upslope. I suppose the brakes squealing and the wheel turning was prodded a little by my smug, "I've seen your new granddaughter and you haven't." Mostly, though, it was the pull of that baby in the birthing room only four minutes away.

David and I, with son Joel, the family cinematographer, headed into the New Mothers and Infants Ward, with the camcorder capturing every word. My husband bent his gray head over that pink bundle and—ah, yes—fell in love. Right on the spot. And I am not one bit jealous that there's another woman in his life. Preparing to dress for work, the day our grandchild was three days old, after having again abandoned another evening of to-do schemes to hold the baby, he announced, "I am a happy man."

Oh, that all babies born into this world were surrounded by this kind of love, that there were none who were cold or mistreated or resented or hungry or abandoned.

And oh, that Christians understood that the church is a birthing room, that the church is a place where life is encouraged in the middle of this death-camp world. The church must be a place where we can do spiritual labor within its shelter, a place where the agony of becoming is overseen by experts and awaited by concerned friends. This church as birthing room should be a place where we participate in one another's travail and where we share joy and exultation when our work is successfully accomplished. The church must be a place where mercy is given before judgment.

You see, we share a common life, and it is a life filled with many births and many deaths. All births should interest us, whether they are physical, emotional, or spiritual. And all deaths should be of concern to us. In the birth chamber of the church we should rejoice with those who rejoice and mourn with those who mourn. At all times we should feel the utter tenderness toward one another that I felt in that midnight hour holding my firstborn granddaughter in my arms.

We must hold one another in the face of all nativities. "To life!" shout the dancers and the actors in the musical *Fiddler on the Roof.* "To life!" should be our communal pledge as well. Then in death, even in death, we will have developed the habit of looking to life. Holding the broken body, we keep life in mind. Paul beautifully explains this paradox to the Corinthians:

> But we have this treasure in earthen vessels, that the excellence of the power may be of God and not of us. We are hard pressed on every side, yet not crushed; we are perplexed, but not in despair; persecuted, but not forsaken, struck down, but not destroyed—always carrying about in the body the dying of the Lord Jesus, that the life of Jesus also may be manifested in our body. For we who live are always delivered to death for Jesus' sake, that the life of Jesus also may be manifested in our mortal flesh.[1]

I'd like to end this chapter with three pietàs, three examples of how the church community can be a birthing room to our society.

THE CHURCH AS A SHELTERING PLACE FOR THE LOST

Anne Lamott paints a picture of the sheltering church in her book *Operating Instructions*. Perhaps because David and I worked in inner-city churches for years, I find that this writer's descriptions bring back into focus the urban incongruities I love and experienced in the neighborhoods of Chicago. Her book is about the first year of her son's life; it is also about her own continued spiritual nativity and about the surprising death from cancer of Lamott's best friend, Peg, a circumstance not in motion at the beginning of the chronicle.

The author writes about a little black church in Marin City, tells how before she stopped drinking she would wander in, mostly because it was near a flea market where she spent time when she was hung over. In a tense, lurking way, she'd hang around the back of the church on Sundays and then leave before the service was over to avoid being touched or hugged or talked to. In a little while she began to participate in the worship and singing. After Anne became sober, she would stay to the end:

> Now I show up and position myself near the door, and everyone has to give me a huge hug—it's like trying to get past the border patrol. Once I asked my priest friend, Bill Rankin, if he really believed in miracles, and he said that all I needed to do was to remember what my life used to be like and what it's like now. He said he thought I ought to change my name to Exhibit A.[2]

Part of the privilege of my life has been to hear stories such as these. The Exhibit A's that I know are too numerous to mention.

People, for the most part, ease into the Christian life. A church that can allow the hung over druggie to slink around the back door without condemnation and lavishly welcome her and her baby born out of wedlock knows the powerful workings of holy love. Holding, lap-type lamentations, mercy, and the patient wait for redemption are hallmarks of this kind of local Christian community.

Lamott paints a poignant picture of all this, and because her own words are so fresh and unencumbered by religious pieties, I quote:

> Anyway, the first Sunday after Sam's birth, I kind of limped in with Peg beside me. I was holding Sam and she was holding my little inflated doughnut seat, and everyone was staring joyfully and almost brokenheartedly at us because they love us so much. I walked, like a ship about to go down, to a seat in the back.
>
> But the pastor said, "Whoa, whoa, not so fast—you come up here and introduce him to his new family."
>
> So I limped up to the little Communion table in the front of the half circle of folding chairs where we sit, and I turned to face everyone. The pain and joy were just overwhelming. I tried to stammer, "This is my son," but my lip was trembling, my whole face was trembling, and everyone was crying.
>
> When I'd first started coming to the church, I couldn't even stand up for half the songs because I'd be so sick from cocaine and alcohol that my head would be spinning, but these people were so confused that they'd thought I was a child of God. Now they've seen me sober for three years, and they saw me through my pregnancy. Only one (white) man in the whole congregation asked me who the father was. Toward the end of my pregnancy, people were stuffing money into my pockets,

> even though a lot of them live on welfare and tiny pensions. They'll sidle up to me, slip a twenty into the pocket of my sweater and dart away.
>
> Anyway, after I introduced Sam to them and sat down on my doughnut seat in the front row with Peg, I really got into the service. The baby was sound asleep in my arms, and I stood for the first hymn feeling very adult—an actual *mother*, for God's sake— only to discover that the doughnut seat was stuck to my bottom, and milk was absolutely pouring out of my breasts. I was not yet secure enough to hold the baby with one hand, so I was cradling him in my arms and couldn't free up either hand to pull the doughnut seat off. So I stood there bent slightly forward, warbling away, with my butt jutting out and ringed by the plastic doughnut.[3]

I cry when I read this, knowing how many souls could be wooed from the flea market to the back door of the church, to the worship, to the singing, then finally to the front row, despite their agonies, if Christians only understood the meaning of pietà.

Pietàs. Shelters for the lost. And a caring community of support for the homeless.

THE CHURCH AS A SUPPORT FOR THE HOMELESS

While attending a fund-raising training conference for not-for-profits in Philadelphia, I met the staff of Bridge of Hope, an unusual outreach that helps homeless mothers and children. Their pamphlet summarizes the underlying difficulty of assisting those cruelly thrust out into the streets: "Homelessness is more than just a housing crisis. It is also a relationship crisis." People not only lose jobs and their shelter, they often lose (or have never established) the networks that provide the ladders to climb out of disaster.

The unique approach of Bridge of Hope is to involve teams of trained mentors, some eight to twelve individuals from local churches, to support networks for the homeless. This team becomes a caring community that provides the sort of personal encouragement committed friends would supply when crisis strikes. Volunteers give friendship, usable household items, and baby-sitting services. Professionals give counseling, and the organization makes skill-training services available and helps find job employment opportunities.

Bridge of Hope seeks to break down the stereotypes regarding the homeless. A homeless woman may be working forty hours a week and struggling to raise two children on her own. But her five-dollar-an-hour pay is simply not enough to put aside a security deposit and the first month's rent. She may be employed twenty-five hours a week with no hope of increased hours and with no medical benefits. She may lack job skills. Homeless women stated in Bridge of Hope's brochure:

> "I never for one moment thought I'd be homeless. I would have laughed if you would have told me two years ago, that today I'd be homeless."
>
> "I was not an alcoholic or drug addict, nor was I mentally ill as the media would have us believe the majority of homeless people are. How could this happen to me?"
>
> "It's like in that movie that was on TV with Lucille Ball. She was a homeless woman. She lived in her car but she appeared high class and all because she was pretty and clean and went into department stores to put on her make-up. You can't tell

simply by looking at someone whether or not they have a home to live in."[4]

A cycle of poverty sucks people into its spiraling descent. Divorce occurs and support payments falter. A job is lost. Catastrophic medical illness strikes. The car breaks down; there is no money to fix it; and the wage earner can't get to work. A child may have a major physical or mental disability and the mother can't leave. The rent goes unpaid. The bank forecloses or the landlord sends an eviction notice.

One mother describes trying to find help for herself and two children, a daughter eleven and an infant sixteen months:

> I thought things could only get better, but I was wrong. I spent my days in class, driving my older daughter back and forth to school (I wanted to keep her in the same school), hoping my 1976 Nova would not fall apart, and frantically and repeatedly calling every agency I could trying to find help.
>
> The people at the housing authority told me they were not accepting applications for low income housing, and even if they were, there is a three to five year waiting list. There were agencies that could provide food or clothing, or help if you are behind on your rent, but none to help you get back on your feet. One agency may have been able to help, but they told me I had not been on welfare long enough to qualify! My goal was to get off assistance and take care of my family myself, not stay on welfare for years. I quickly learned why so many people go from one shelter to another.
>
> September was gone, then October, and I was obsessed with getting us into our own home by the girls' birthdays (in November). But after countless hours of phone calls and endless legwork, I was no closer to getting us out than before. . . .

> I remember very clearly how one night, in our room, while my children slept, I gave up. I totally lost all hope that I could change our situation. In that dark moment of utter despair, I prayed. I admitted to God that I could not do this by myself, and I asked for the Lord's help. I felt such a sense of peace wash over me that I knew the Lord was with me. For the first time in months, I slept well.[5]

A week later, this woman was introduced to the Bridge of Hope outreach; within three weeks, she and her children were moving out of the cycle of homelessness, poverty, and dependency.

Bridge of Hope seeks to serve women and their children who suffer from these cataclysms. The organization provides rental assistance on a decreasing scale for a maximum of nine months, just enough time to enable families to settle into housing, get a regular salary established, and receive the benefits of the support network of mentors. In addition to establishing and training mentor groups and raising funds to supply rent subsidies, Bridge of Hope coordinates service planning, connects families with existing social services, and provides case management for twelve to eighteen months.

Most homeless women who come to Bridge of Hope have lived in thirty-day emergency shelters, campgrounds, crowded boarding houses, or they have doubled up with friends and family in cramped apartments.

The *Philadelphia Inquirer* focused on the life of one woman:

> At seven, eight, nine months pregnant, she was sleeping on park benches in West Chester and sneaking into college dorms to take showers. Her $200-a-day coke habit had "snorted,

> smoked and shot" up all her rent money and left her on the streets.
>
> Today, she rents her own apartment, with yellow ruffled curtains in the kitchen and a Snoopy magnet on the refrigerator. She has a steady job packing fried chicken in a poultry plant. She is no longer on welfare or food stamps. She is raising a healthy daughter on her own. What made the difference . . . was an innovative program that seeks to give homeless people what they need most: not a bed in a shelter, but a support system, a community, a family.[6]

The success of Bridge of Hope is that the program matches homeless women who want help with groups of individuals and families who want to help, a unique approach that seeks to provide secure permanent housing and financial self-sufficiency, and to meet physical, emotional, spiritual, and social needs. The bridge, of course, is this caring scaffolding that links the resources of the local church to the neglected needy in the community.

One of the women assisted out of homelessness by the work of Bridge of Hope stated, "I was told that if every church in Pennsylvania 'adopted' one homeless family, there would be no more homeless people in the state. What a challenge!"

THE CHURCH AS A REFUGE FOR THOSE IN THE VALLEY OF THE SHADOW

Someone in my extended family counted one day and determined that there are seventeen ordained ministers in the three generations that extend from the lineage of my great-grandmother, Cornelia Goins Burton. It is true. There are a lot of clergy types around. My husband is an ordained minister. My brother is an ordained minister. My father was an ordained minister (although of the musical stripe, a minister of music). My brother-in-law is an ordained minister. And my daughter's husband was on his way to ordination at Asbury Seminary after taking a degree in theater at Miami University of Ohio when David called both of them to come back to Chicago to be a part of our television ministry.

Through the years, I've concluded that one of the basic premises that those in pastoral ministry must recognize is the capacity to walk alongside people in the joyful celebrations and the terrible crises of their everyday living. The pastor who fails to understand the powerful holding influence of spiritual presence— of being there for the wedding, for the fiftieth anniversary celebration, for the wake and the visitation and the funeral—does not understand or is not called to pastoral ministry. He or she may be a great preacher, a remarkable administrator, and a wise forecaster of trends in the culture and the church's relationship to those shifts. But at its essence, pastoring is representing Christ, standing in physically for him at the cycles of life events that occur day in and day out and have existed since the original man and woman formed an embryo society.

That quality of being there, that sense of physical presence, is holding at its most sublime, particularly in the moments of life's deepest pains. The pastor of children's ministries of the First Evangelical Free Church of Rockford, Illinois, walked me through a moment in the life of that congregation that recapitulates in real life the meaning of these last pietàs: Anne Lamont's testament to a little black community church that took in a white woman in recovery and protected her during the birth of her infant, and the Bridge of Hope that rescues homeless women and children.

One Friday morning, word spread through Rockford that a little girl had drowned while on a fifth-grade outing in a local forest preserve. She had fallen from the canoe that her own teacher had been paddling; the canoe struck a submerged log, tipping over and trapping the child under water. It took twenty minutes to recover her lifeless body. For any community, the death of a child is a shock and a horrifying reminder of the fragility of our supposed security.

As the news went out and the name of the child, Mindy Robertson, and her family became known, a call went to the office of the church. A member of the congregation recognized the family, her husband sat next to the father at work. She reported a short conversation the two men had exchanged about church attendance. The family had previously gone to First Free, but they were not presently involved in a local congregation. That meant they would not be covered by a ministering presence at their moment of greatest need.

The receptionist typed the family's name into the computer, and she called the pastor of children's ministry, Jim Rosene, because of the age of the child and the family's previous attendance at First Free. Though Jim tried, he couldn't place the child, but around 2:00 the afternoon of the drowning, he phoned the family and got the answering machine. Naturally, he left a message, expressing his dismay over these terrible circumstances, left his home phone number, and offered any assistance the family might need. He then called a friend who is an emergency room doctor in one of the local hospitals. That hospital hadn't handled the case, but the doctor located the emergency room that had received the child's body and filled Jim Rosene in on details, just in case the father returned his call.

On Saturday morning, Jim Rosene was at the church early, around 6:30; he checked the accounts of the drowning in the local newspaper and still didn't recognize the family or the child. That bothered him. If the fifth grader had been a part of his children's program, he was sure he would remember her. And if he didn't remember her, she must not have been involved recently. It troubled him to think that the family might be between churches at a time when they desperately needed pastoral care. He contacted a few more people who might know the family, and then he phoned a funeral home to inquire as to whether arrangements for the burial were being handled there. He was steered to the appropriate place and, again, he let the director know that he would be more than happy to give pastoral assistance. If the family was being ministered to by another local church, that was wonderful; but if not, the staff and people at First Free wanted to do whatever they could to help.

At 1:30 in the afternoon the father returned Pastor Rosene's phone call. The two talked a while; Jim Rosene assured him of the fact that the staff and members of the church were lifting the family up to God in loving concern. The father said that the middle daughter in the family often attended the Sunday school of another church and that they would see if that pastor could handle the funeral. Just in case, Jim Rosene checked to see if the auditorium at First Free would be available for the funeral services; if John Robertson did call back to say that the other pastor was out of town and that the building couldn't be used, Pastor Rosene would be able to offer the facilities and ministrations of First Free.

At 3:30 that afternoon the father called again. "Would you be willing to do the service?"

At that point, Jim Rosene secured the sanctuary and the fellowship hall, and another pastor on the staff took on the responsibility of organizing the meal after the funeral and the graveside ceremonies.

At 7:00 on Saturday evening, the day after the drowning, Jim Rosene went to Mindy Robertson's home where all the extended family, grandparents, aunts, uncles, cousins were gathering. It was a desperate moment. The pastor still didn't recognize the mother or father, and he frankly says he had no idea as to what to do. He is a children's pastor, after all; he was called to deal with burgeoning, riotous life, not death. People were weeping; the kids were running around. He met the mother who was feeling that somehow it was all her fault. The father came and talked a little bit about their child. He showed videos and photographs. Mindy had been involved in the church's activities.

The next day, Sunday, was Mother's Day. By this time, the deaconesses had rallied and were making plans to carry out the traditional services of their calling. The family's name had been in the newspaper, and people were much in prayer and in empathy over this great pain and distress and loss. There was a child dedication service that morning; Sunday school, children's church, three services, the normal crises and responsibilities that occur on every Sunday morning. It was 4:00 before Pastor Rosene was able to call the Robertsons.

John Robertson apologized; he had forgotten to tell Jim that there was a family viewing at the funeral home that evening. Could he be there? At 6:20 Jim walked into the funeral parlor to be among a group of people filled with tears and grief. But this time, because of the congregation's prayers, he was filled with an inner strength to minister that he had never felt before.

He started talking with individual family members, prayed several times, and a bonding began to grow between them.

On Monday morning, Jim Rosene was very concerned for the classmates of Mindy Robertson. He slipped over to the school just to see how everyone was doing. As soon as the staff knew who he was, he was welcomed and taken to the classroom where he discovered that some ten to twelve social workers and counselors were mobilizing to deal with the process of helping children through the shock of the death of a friend their age. Two other pastors of a church down the street from the school were already present and ready to be utilized however they were needed. Jim Rosene said teachers and the principal repeatedly told him how much this was all appreciated. "I introduced myself to the class but let the other pastor talk about what a funeral is and how to act at a funeral."

Jim Rosene met the teacher who had been in the canoe from which Mindy had fallen and recognized his profound distress. "I would like to say I understand what you are feeling, and how responsible you must hold yourself for this death, but I really can't." However, one of the other pastors at First Free, the junior-high pastor, had suffered a similar event when a student under his supervision had died in an accident. Arrangements were begun to bring the two together.

When Jim left the school, he visited the family again and spent forty-five minutes with them. At this time the hard questions were beginning to rise. "Was it God's will?" Jim Rosene said simply, "I don't know."

By Tuesday, the day of the funeral, the staff at First Free were organized to help the family and the mourners go through this day. Due to media attention, two staff members were appointed to answer phones and handle the press. During the visitation, one secretary stopped counting at twelve hundred people who passed to view the child's body in the casket. A member of the staff steered the family to a side door where they could avoid the crowd and go to a private office. Rosene prayed with them, and they went together into the 2:00 service. Seven hundred eighty-five people attended the funeral.

Nothing is more difficult for a minister than helping a family deal with the loss of a child; and perhaps nothing is more challenging than preaching the sermon at a child's funeral. One must be concerned not only about the family, but about all those who attend, many of whom are not church people and who too are asking the hard questions, "If there is a God, why does he allow this suffering?"

A friend of the family sang; an aunt of the child wrote and read a letter from the family; some eulogies were shared. Then Pastor Rosene rose to give the sermon.

"I'm a children's pastor," he said. "So let me tell you a story. That's what I do." And he told the story from the New Testament about Jesus calming the storm. The disciples couldn't handle this storm, he said. Though some of them were fishermen, the wind and thrashing waters seemed to be beyond their skill. Certainly someone in that rocking boat questioned, "Where's Jesus?" And they discovered he was in the boat with them. Then, Jim Rosene looked at the mother and father, their beloved child dead. "Certainly, you must be asking in the midst of this terrible storm, 'Where's Jesus?' I am here to remind you that he's right in the boat with you."

Mrs. Robertson had told Jim Rosene that when Mindy woke in the middle of the night afraid, she would quote Proverbs 3:5–6 to her. "Trust in the LORD with all your heart, / And lean not on your own understanding; / In all your ways acknowledge Him, / And He shall direct your paths."

Jim Rosene, the children's pastor, walked down from the platform, held the mother's hand, and quoted this passage to her, "Trust in the LORD with all your heart. . . ." As he closed in prayer, he grasped the father's hand as well.

I can only imagine the picture this minister gave to those who came to attend the funeral of that child: to parents and grade-school friends, to teachers, to sympathetic citizens of Rockford, to the press. After the interment, when the family gathered back at the church for the meal prepared by the deaconesses, one of the grandfathers said to Pastor Rosene, "You don't know what that sermon meant to me. I am filled with such peace now."

At various points the media caught Jim Rosene. One reporter stuck a microphone in his face and asked, "How do you tell children about death?"

The children's pastor replied, and the newspapers printed, "So many children believe in heaven. So we talk about Jesus. We talk about how Jesus wants to be with them in heaven. Frankly, we don't know why God allowed this to happen. We don't know why God didn't intervene. But we do know that Mindy is with Jesus."

After the funeral, Pastor Rosene took a phone call from a woman who was not a member of the First Evangelical Free congregation. Out of the great sympathy of her heart, she wanted to help bear some of the expenses that had been incurred by the death and funeral of this child. Jim sensed that she thought the church would charge for their services. He had to explain to her that, of course, the funeral home had fees, but that any of the ministrations provided by the church were given free of charge, in the name of Christ. And then he said, "You see this is what we do. When there is need, we are there to help. Indeed, this is what we should do best."

I agree with Jim Rosene, the children's pastor at First Evangelical Free Church of Rockford, Illinois. This is what we do, we Christians. We take the broken body into our arms and we hold it. We surround the grieving parents with loving protection and service. We explain the meaning of death to classmates and prepare food for the extended family after the internment. We handle the press so that their questions can be answered and the mourners will not be distressed. We say again what they already know but need to hear from another in these seasons of sorrow, "I don't have the answers to all the difficult questions. But I know that in this storm Christ is in the boat with you. Trust in the Lord."

This is what we do. This is what we do.

We go to those in their hours of deepest need.

Mercy.

Christ, have mercy.

Pietà.

Part Four

The Final Pietàs

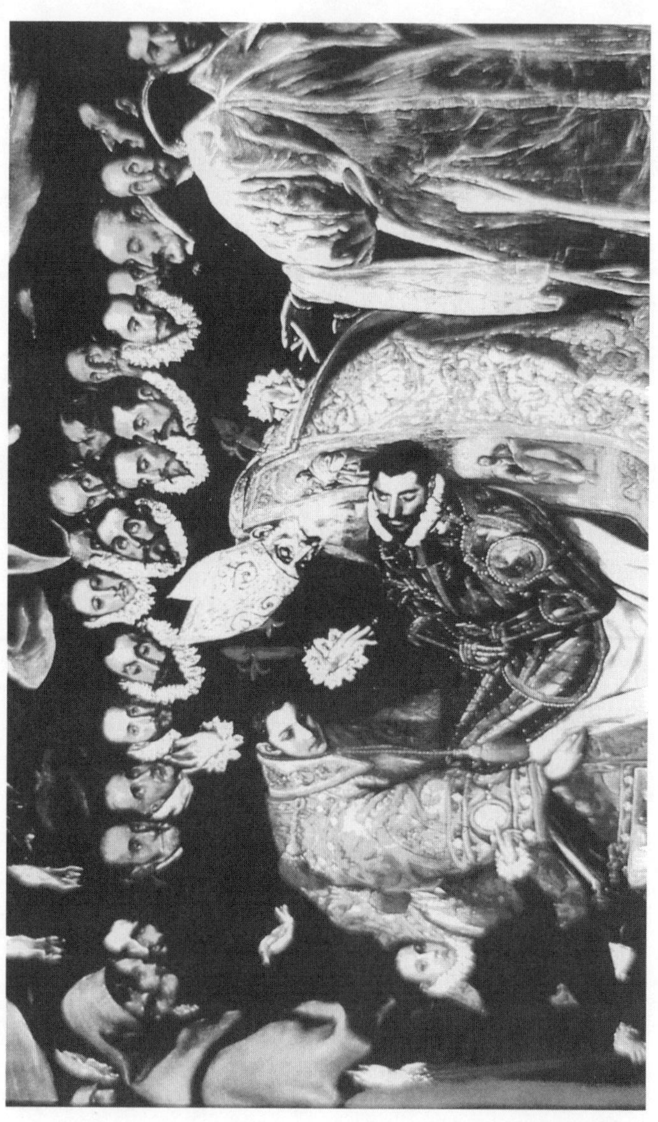

What a blessing for a whole community to embrace the life and death of a person for their acts on earth. And what a blessing for the living soul now in heaven, embraced by the saints, the angels, and Jesus himself. *El Greco,* The Burial of the Count of Orgaz, *painting, 1586, Toledo, Spain, Photo courtesy of Corbis-Bettmann*

Chapter Thirteen

The Final Deaths

For three days in November 1996, the secular media in Chicago conducted an unintentional evangelistic campaign. The occasion for this incongruous event was the death, the visitation, the funeral, and the burial of Cardinal Joseph Bernardin. Regular television programming was preempted for hours as television crews sat outside the residence where his body rested in a private chapel. They videotaped the entourage as the casket was transported to Holy Name Cathedral where the cardinal had served as pastor; they interviewed people in the long lines stretching around the block, the devoted waiting in the bitter cold to pay their last respects. Newspaper editors assigned pages of copy; special editions were printed. The cardinal's remarkable life and death were the focus of popular talk shows. A whole city was in mourning.

Why? I wondered. What was it about this church leader that inspired a normally skeptical press corps to bow its knees in homage? Granted, Chicago is a city of 8 million with an estimated Catholic population of 2.4 million, a significant percentage. But I have lived here all my life, and Catholic archbishops come and go. I have never seen this outpouring of local favor over the life of any man, whether a political leader or a business tycoon or a community organizer. For days, I sat in front of my television mesmerized by the embrace this sophisticated midwestern city was extending to one clergyman.

Over and over stories of kindness and goodness were told as examples of his Christian faith. Finally, someone had modeled what the press felt a Christian leader should be. And the more the journalists prodded and interviewed, the more the testimonies accumulated as to the integrity of his life. No matter your position—a Protestant with an anti-Catholic bias, an adamant nonbeliever or agnostic, a disfranchised former communicant with an ax to grind against the church—it was clear to all that something uncommon was happening during those three days in Chicago.

Indeed, I began to watch a pietà form as that metropolitan area (led by the media) encircled his memory with accolades. It is a matter of public record that for three days the secular communications industry, of all things, clearly defined the parameters of Christian life: A Christian is someone who is charitable, who exercises power with humility, who is truthful and walks in integrity, who takes difficult stands on moral issues, who works for justice, who tirelessly seeks reconciliation, who forgives his enemies, who conducts disagreements with civility, who faces death without fear. For those who had ears to hear, all of this was what it meant to follow in the footsteps of Christ. I found myself joking, "Well, all that's lacking is an altar call!"

Soft spoken, but intellectually brilliant, the cardinal worked for reconciliation not only among his own Catholic clerics but also among other clergy of the area. One rabbi interviewed on television, after Bernardin's death, said, "I trusted him. In some sense, I felt as though he was my pastor."[1]

I began to realize there was an unusual moral presence among us when Bernardin headed the American Bishops Encyclical, which propounded the Consistent Ethic of Life. I have been long disturbed myself by the evangelical pro-life movement because it seems to truncate its effect by applying its energies only to the single issue of abortion. What about the wasted lives of children in urban centers? What about the rape of the earth? Aren't these pro-life causes also? The Catholic Bishops Encyclical proposed a context in which to view a far-ranging set of modern moral issues. In an address at Fordham University, Bernardin explained:

> The dominant cultural fact, present in both modern warfare and modern medicine, which induces a sharper awareness of the fragility of human life is our technology. . . . The essential question in the technological challenge is this: In an age when we can do almost anything, how do we decide what we ought to do? The even more demanding question is that in a time when we can do anything technologically, how do we decide morally what we never should do?
>
> Asking these questions along the spectrum of life from womb to tomb creates the need for a consistent ethic of life. For the spectrum of life cuts across the issues of genetics, abortion, capital punishment, modern warfare and the care of the terminally ill. These are all distinct problems, enormously complicated, and deserving individual treatment. No single answer and no simple responses will solve them.[2]

In the light of these commendable positions, a young man, Stephen Cook, shook the Chicago community in November 1993 with the public accusation of sexual abuse. He claimed to have recovered a repressed memory of an incident when Bernardin was Cincinnati's archbishop. The press, of course, entered into a period of reporter frenzy. And why not? We are daily distressed by the disclosures of corruptness in high places, of supposedly holy leaders driven by the demons of addictions and lusts. Bernardin's simple response was, "I can assure you that all my life I have led a chaste and celibate life." But the accusation was potentially debilitating toward a man some felt might be the first American elected pope. The cardinal himself confessed that his greatest fear had been to be the victim of some unfounded accusation.

In time Steven Cook recanted his charges, and it was then that the press, at first ready to dismember a hypocritical churchman, now became witness to the profound parameters of Christian charity. A year after the painful accusations, Bernardin became aware that his accuser was dying of AIDS. Flying to Philadelphia, the cardinal spent two hours with the young man:

> I began by telling Steven that the only reason for requesting the meeting was to bring closure to the traumatic events of last winter by personally letting him know that I harbored no ill feelings toward him and to pray with him for his physical and spiritual well-being. He replied that he wanted to meet with me to apologize for the embarrassment and hurt he had caused. In other words, we both sought reconciliation.[3]

Obviously, here was a spiritual leader who never forgot the soul of the matter, and this concern was noticed, then dutifully reported by the press.

> Steven's apology was simple, direct, deeply moving. I accepted his apology. I told him that I had prayed for him every day and would continue to pray for his health and peace of mind. . . . I also told him that while I would not want to go through such a humiliating experience again, nonetheless it had contributed to my own spiritual growth and had made me more compassionate. Before Steven left, he told me that a big burden had been lifted from him. . . . He felt healed and was at peace.[4]

Stephen Cook died before Cardinal Bernardin died, but the way this incident was conducted was proof positive to cynical journalists that Christianity was well and flourishing in some small pockets of American culture. From that moment on, for the major media players in Chicago, it was as though the man could do no wrong.

In June 1995 the city was made aware that Bernardin had been diagnosed with pancreatic cancer. It was then that we all had the rare opportunity of watching a public figure, a person of faith, learn to embrace his dying and his death. The press quoted a pastoral letter, a monumental demonstration of quiet honesty and courage:

> When I entered the Loyola University Medical Center, my life had been turned completely upside down by the totally unexpected news that what I had been experiencing as a healthy body was, in fact, housing a dangerous, aggressive cancer. The time since the diagnosis, surgery and postoperative radiation

> and chemotherapy has led me into a new dimension of my life-long journey of faith. . . .
>
> I came to believe in a new way that the Lord would walk with me through this journey of illness that would take me from a former way of life into a new manner of living.
>
> Nevertheless, during my convalescence I found the nights to be especially long, a time for various fears to surface. I sometimes found myself weeping, something I seldom did before. And I came to realize how much of what consumes our daily life truly is trivial and insignificant.[5]

The cancer recurred and a whole city was drawn into the grace of his dying by the press. Over the months, through morning and nightly news, every now and then, we watched him make his farewells. He took a last trip to Rome to meet with the Pope; his own congregation at Holy Name Cathedral were prepared; priests were gathered for final words and final blessings.

A month before his death, he spoke at Mundelein Seminary. This was also recorded in newspapers and repeated again and again in the days surrounding his funeral:

> Through all of this, my brothers and sisters, I am at peace and I can only account for that by looking upon it as a gift from God. People have asked me, "How can you explain this peace?" Three things come to mind. First of all, you really have to trust the Lord. At an intellectual level, we do. But at a much deeper, personal and emotional level, you have to learn to trust. If you don't have that trust, there's no way to have that peace of mind. The second thing is that if you believe in the Lord and trust the Lord, you should be able to see death as a friend, and not as an enemy. If the first is right and the second

is right, the third follows: You have to let go. That letting go is not the easiest thing in the world.[6]

It is reported that Cardinal Joseph Bernardin assigned his funeral to the hands of trusted coworkers, certain they would do "what was appropriate." Carefully orchestrated, each element was pregnant with symbolic meaning, carefully explained to a watching public by well-chosen liturgists, color commentators if you will, Catholic theologians appointed to their tasks by some savvy media expert in the diocesan headquarters. But most symbolic, perhaps, were the lines of mourners, including the curious, who waited along the path that the funeral cortege took from Holy Name Cathedral to Mount Carmel Cemetery in suburban Hillside, a route that wound in and out through blocks of the city. Eloquently, the *Tribune* reporter captured the feel of Chicago:

> It will move past the squat union halls, ghettos and peaceful city park lagoons, small storefront Missionary Baptist chapels with faded, hand-painted signs and great stone Catholic churches and Catholic schools abandoned to black Protestants. . . . it will wind through downtown streets, past men in rich Italian suits and homeless women holding cups begging quarters. . . . It will go through a Near West Side that is reshaping itself. . . . And then the larger West Side of broken windows, junk cars in the vacant lots, men in the streets, old women hobbling, their legs wrapped in beige elastic bandages.[7]

There are unique moments when whole communities bend to honor righteous men, and there is a lesson to be learned in this by us all. Righteousness, they say, is its own reward. Our culture hungers for authentic goodness. We have had enough of the antihero. Bernardin's death reminds me that when we do the work of God in the world we are loved, often by more than we know.

But the response of the city of Chicago is also a picture of a communal pietà, a whole community embracing one it loved in the moment of death. Here was a living pietà, again—months of the holding of a well-loved leader as he faced the final dying for anyone who had eyes to see.

In 1586 El Greco, "the Greek," completed a commission from the parish priest of the Church of Santo Tome titled *The Burial of the Count of Orgaz.* "My sublime work," the artist himself called the painting, and, indeed, the recent century has verified this to be one of his masterpieces. Doug Kracht, a friend who put aside his missionary responsibilities for a few days to become my art guide, and I stood beneath the wall in the tiny chapel in Toledo, Spain, and gazed up at this magnificent piece. Breaking with the artistic forms of the age (one critic calls El Greco the impressionist of the waning Renaissance), this work transcends the material and in some hard-to-define way feels "spiritual" to the observing eye.

After returning home, I studied replications, chased down and purchased a copy of *El Greco: The Burial of the Count of Orgaz* by Francisco Calvo Serraller, took notes, attended an art institute lecture on El Greco, and I am only just beginning to crack its meaning in order to explain its power. The painting essentially commemorates the funeral of Don Gonzalo Ruiz, lord of the township of Oraz, prothonotary of Castile, a man given to deep devotion and acts of charity, a true benefactor of the church. It shows the officials of the town lowering his armor-clad form into the grave. Another body in death surrounded by supporters and admirers.

However, El Greco has captured something vastly beyond the record of the funeral of a remarkable man. Above the human forms in the painting, which fills one wall of the chapel, above the line of black-clad attending priests and the mourners and the dead body of the count, above all these funereal dignitaries, is represented the saints of the past, now living, prophets and apostles and disciples arching to a vault, and at the apex of the painting a triumphant and living Christ.

In the realm of the celestial, as contrasted to the earthly, all is splendid—the magnificent swirling of heavenly clouds, the almost surreal colors, the dazzling luminosity. Here the angels and Mary, the mother, John the Baptist, and all the witnesses, now lively, turn their faces toward Christ, fix their eyes on him in adoration and wonder.

The more I study this work, the more it means; but on its most substantial level it opens to me a reality that exists, that I rarely experience and mostly forget. That reality is that the supernatural good is always present and always surrounds me. It is always able to surprise me and break into my ordinary time. There is a heavenly kingdom that arches over my daily living, and it extends eternally beyond my finite existence. Like the crest of El Greco's masterpiece, there is a great surrounding cloud of witnesses engaged in the unending contemplation of my Lord and Savior, the living and resurrected Christ.

I am in my fifties, and it has become clear to me that I must seriously be about the business of preparing my soul for death. I want a soul enlarged enough to meet its Creator with joy, and

I do not, in that final day of dying, want to be ashamed of the narrowness, of the waste, of the cramped or tortured state of my spiritual being. I want to go into heaven with a shining soul. I want to gleefully join that celestial crowd. I want to eagerly turn my eyes toward Christ. I want to consider death, when it comes, as a friend. So I must remember, must continually remind myself: There is another place, another time, another and better world.

All the little deaths prepare me to pass through the last death. And I truly believe, because I have discovered so many pietàs here on earth (and all the artists and poets and mystics remind me), that when I make that final and, to some, fearful passage I will not be alone. Hopefully I will see, like the viewer who stands in front of El Greco's masterpiece in the little chapel of Santo Tome in Toledo, that something greater than death is always with us. Something larger even than the life I know and understand. Something vaster than my dreams or imaginings. When I die, I too will be welcomed into that final embrace, into the great enfolding arms of mercy. And I will finally know, at a level my crimped and incapacitated heart can never here attain; I will know love.

I must never forget that in all the final deaths mercy is always near.

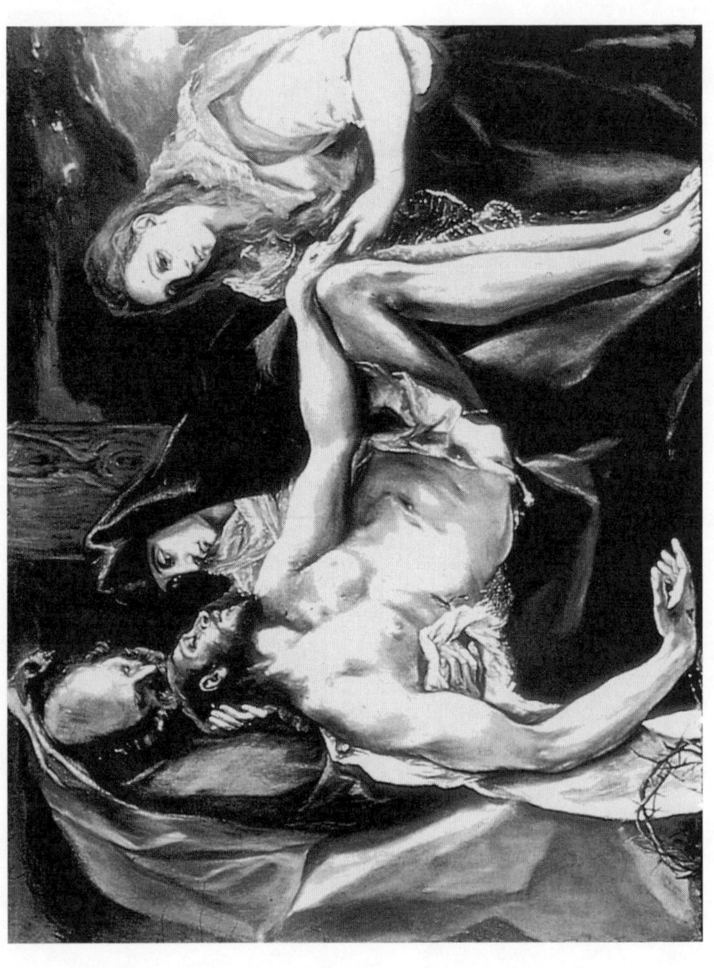

Christ's death, a painful tragedy, but a necessary one. What greater gift could God give us than his Son's life and mercy? What greater gift can we give others than that same mercy?
El Greco, Pietà, *painting, Photo courtesy of Corbis-Bettmann*

Chapter Fourteen

THE FULFILLMENT OF LONGING

In 1994 and the spring of 1995 a wave of open confession, repentance, and cleansing swept through many Christian colleges. At 10:00 o'clock on the evening of March 21, we received a phone call. It was from Jim Warren, host of *Prime Time,* the Moody Network afternoon drive show.

"David, has anyone notified you? A revival has broken out among the students at Wheaton College. The group has grown so they are moving tonight's meeting to a new auditorium—to the College Church across the street. If you can, I think you'd better come."

Within a half hour, David and I were dressed and sitting in the balcony of the College Church where hundreds of young people were gathered. The classic accounts of revival have been a lifetime study for my husband. He's read about it countless times, painted the historical pictures of those moments in books and in broadcasts and from pulpits. David has described the past in order to teach the classic signs of every true revival. He has attempted to create a hunger in the hearts of readers and listeners for this visitation of the Almighty. But never, in all his fifty-eight years, had he actually experienced the pouring out of God's presence in this way.

A gentle, quiet spirit filled the sanctuary. Young people waited patiently in line to speak alternately at two microphones. "I must confess to you and to God . . ." many of them began. And then in brokenness and in tears, they gave forth their most hidden secret sins. "I've hated this school, this student body, and I beg forgiveness." "I'm addicted to pornography." "I'm guilty of the sin of arrogance." "I've mocked God, mocked the Holy Spirit, mocked the workings of God." "I have been sexually impure." "I've lusted after men [women] on this campus." "I've hardened my heart to spiritual truths."

After each confession, other students gathered around the repentant sinner in loving prayer, absorbing that painful vulnerability within a circle of care. In a sense, the circle absorbed the sin, hid it from the eyes of the watchers. Those merciful friends covered the confessor in the same way that God covers each of us when we confess our sins to him. Another and another student went to the microphone, all of them eventually embraced. Small groups of praying students huddled in aisles, in hallways, in pews, in the narthex. A group would break, their covering prayers completed, and all would return to their seats, the repentant student glowing with joy, tears of release shining in his or her eyes.

Here was a picture of the loving-kindness of God shown forth in his body, "But love covers all sins."[1] The presence of the merciful Christ was overwhelmingly among us. "This is a marvelous work of God," interpreted Chaplain Steve Kellogg. "There is no other way to explain this. We are undergoing a holy cleansing."

There was another act of mercy that evening. I remember sitting in the balcony of the auditorium and thinking: *What a gift of God for David to be here to see this outpouring on this particular night!* That very day, Tuesday, March 21, my husband had taped the last broadcast of *The Chapel of the Air,* figuratively closing the door on a fifty-five-and-one-half-year history of fruitful radio ministry. We had actually been sitting in his study considering the emotional impact of this on him. Admittedly, it had been a solitary ending, just David and our engineer. No cheers. No hurrahs. No farewells.

Sometime in the weeks before, my recovering workaholic husband had said, "What's wrong with me? I feel like I'm on the verge of tears all the time."

And I explained that it was natural and normal to feel grief at the mercy death of a ministry into which he had invested twenty years of diligence and passion.

But David's passion was not so much for the broadcast itself, nor for the public ministry; the ministry's national medium was a base to sound the alarm for his intense prophetic calling: "Make way! Make way! Prepare the way of the Lord!" Truly, for years his was one of the few lonely voices crying in the wilderness of American church culture. Media experts, the head of our radio agency, continually warned David that a revival message was not the felt need of the Christian radio audience. I sat in the meetings and heard them say it to him. David wasn't sounding an alarm about the family. He wasn't lobbying for political action. He was not conducting witch-hunts against other ministries. He didn't use the familiar evangelical style of verse-by-verse Bible exposition. He wasn't emphasizing end-time prophecy. He was calling for spiritual revitalization, life coming back again into the Christians and the churches of this land. His determined creativity found thousands of ways to say essentially the same thing without developing negative listener attrition: revival, renewal, restoration, revitalization. Over and over. Again and again. Discontented with the influence of words alone, he also developed the response tools to help people experience little touches of this dramatic revived life.

Our public lives as well as our private lives were dominated with this passion, a passion I was convinced might never find fulfillment.

Christian recording artist Steve Camp sings a song titled "There's Mercy in the Wilderness." For David, certainly, this moment was an example of God's great mercy. We sat in that holy sanctuary the night of the day of his last taping and watched the fulfillment of his longing. It was the first time in nineteen years that he didn't have to leave early, hurry home, stay up all night, or rise before dawn to start, prepare, or finish another broadcast. Suddenly, by God's design, he was free to really attend to the new work breaking forth before his very eyes.

Mercy in the Wilderness

(lyrics from the song by Steve Camp/Rob Frazier)

But He knows the way that I take;
When He has tested me, I shall come forth as gold. . . .
I have not departed from the commandment of His lips;
I have treasured the words of His mouth
More than my necessary food.[2]

Every day that I walk with You
You break me down and You make me new.
Though my faith is tried, this I know is true
There is mercy in the wilderness.

Through the valley deep and the mountain high
You have been my strength and Your Word my guide.
I have known Your grace through the tears I've cried
There is mercy in the wilderness.

In the barren place where the hard winds blow
Oh my flesh cries out, "Lord refresh my soul!"

Oh the Lord is kind
And the Lord is good;
He is faithful to His children.
Through the fire and flood
He has with me stood
He gives mercy in the wilderness.

Oh the chastening of the Father's hand
Yields the peaceful fruit of righteousness.
Though our hope is born in sorrow there'll be joy at last
There is mercy in the wilderness.[3]

AFTERWORD

"Hey, Mom," called my son Joel, the producer of our television show. "An entertainment magazine had an interview with Nicholas Cage about the new film in which he stars." This film, *Con Air,* had been advertised on television; it is a typical Hollywood pyrotechnic-maniacal blow-'em-up-blast-'em-apart macho blood-and-guts sort of action film. Exactly the kind I hate.

Joel continued, "Cage said that he interpreted his character with more of a spiritual bent. During one scene he holds a dying buddy in his arms, in the form of the pietà. You might want to look into that."

Once a collector, always a collector. But now even family and friends are on the hunt. I suppose I will be collecting these pictures of mercy for the rest of my life.

After speaking for a week in Germany for the Protestant Women of the Chapel, an arm of the U.S. Armed Forces Office of the Chaplaincy, I traveled alone to Florence, Italy, and spent a week roaming to my heart's delight. Between the travel allowance and honorarium, I could spend a month in Europe (if I mooched off generous friends and friends of friends). I wanted especially to see Michelangelo's *Florentine Pietà* at the Museo dell'Opera del Duomo, just across from the great cathedral.

Early one chill November morning, I traipsed through the rush-hour traffic and arrived just as the museum was opening.

The *Florentine Pietà* is on a large domed stairway landing. One look and I was stunned. Carved out of a conelike triangle of marble, this sculptured group stood in start contrast to the *Pietà* at St. Peter's in Rome. Sculpted in the artist's old age (his late seventies and early eighties), the work was not for a patron or commission; Vasari, the biographer, indicates it was for Michelangelo's own tomb.[1] At first glance my immediate thought was, *This is a Protestant pietà*.

One is never sure how these flashes come. My intuitive way of knowing often scans faster than my rationality. So an extended "reading" of the sculpture further affirmed the initial assessment. The figure of the dead Christ is vertical, as though having just been taken from the cross. And Christ is central, indeed, and dominating. A Mary is on each side, but not overpowering in drawing the eye of the viewer. The mother, unfinished, is actually a little behind her son.

Extended research uncovered scholarship that insisted that Michelangelo underwent a Protestant-type of conversion during the later years of his life and that his art, beginning with the painted murals of *Last Judgment* on the altar wall of the Sistine Chapel, spoke this forth for any who had eyes to read it. Charles de Tolnay, in his life story of the artist, says, "From the point of view of religious history, then, the final version of the *Last Judgment* can be considered as a remarkable expression of the fundamental doctrine of the Italian Reformation."[2]

This Reformation movement reached Naples with the arrival of Juan Valdes who came from Spain around 1531. In the Naples Circle, which included a narrow gathering of men and women, religious thinkers, and nobility drawn from high ecclesiastical and secular society, the *Institutes* of Calvin were studied in

1536–37.[3] Michelangelo, concerned as he approached the later years of his life with the salvation of his soul, gravitated to these influencers who strongly held to belief in the words of Paul, "Therefore we conclude that a man is justified by faith apart from the deeds of the law."[4] The earlier proclamations of that flaming reformer priest, Savonarola, whose sermons from the pulpits of Florence had so deeply influenced the youthful Michelangelo, now cojoined with Italy's most stimulating religious dialogue.[5] Before the priest's martyrdom, the same concept of justification had been earlier expressed in his *Trattato dell'Umilta*.[6]

Michelangelo came under the tutelage of Vittoria Colonna, the marchessa de Pescara, an intellectual woman of great spiritual stature and a member of the Naples Circle. One of her contemporaries, Cardinal Giberti, wrote, "Not only does she surpass all other women, but she also seems to show the gravest and most famous men the guiding light to the haven of salvation."[7] In one of his letters to her, Michelangelo writes, "[I have] understood and see that the grace of God cannot be bought and that to hold it in disregard is a very great sin."[8]

This same thread winds its way through his later writings, from a poem of that time: "O flesh, O blood, O wood, O extreme suffering, / through you may my sin be made just."[9] A sonnet of 1552 reads:

> The course of my long life hath reached at last,
> In fragile bark o'er a tempestuous sea,
> The common harbor where must rendered be
> Account of all the actions of the past.
> The impassioned fantasy, that, vague and vast,

Made art an idol and a king to me,
Was an illusion, and but vanity
Were the dreams that lured me and harassed,
The dreams of love, that were so sweet of yore—
What are they now, when two deaths may be mine,
One sure, and one forecasting its alarms?
Painting and sculpture satisfy no more
The soul now turning to the Love Divine,
That oped, to embrace us, on the cross its arms.[10]

I am indebted to the research of Dr. John Zimmerman who in his dissertation project writes:

> To sum up the evidence, while Michelangelo was concluding his work of the *Last Judgment* there was a sudden and dramatic shift in his other artistic expressions. His drawings became explicitly Christ-centered. His poetry incorporated Valdesian concepts. He had found his spiritual community in the Circle of Hope through a deeply moving relationship with Vittoria. By the time Pope Paul III was making arrangements to decorate the Pauline Chapel with the *Conversion of Paul*, commissioned October 12, 1541, Michelangelo had certainly arrived at the conviction this work would become his personal witness to a conversion. . . . In the case of Michelangelo this personal confession is to be found reflected in every painting, sculpture and drawing produced after 1541.[11]

At that time, the artist was sixty-six years of age.

Historically, the Counter-Reformation was soon to sweep into Italy upon the heels of the Reformation. A papal bull reestablished the Inquisition to combat the threat of Protestantism, which immediately resulted in an atmosphere of "heresy hunting" in the Italian peninsula. Juan Valdes had died in 1540; remaining leaders of the Reformation movement were summoned to Rome for examination, and they fled across the Alps. The rest renounced their positions, including Vittoria Colonna, who, justifiably fearful of excommunication, died herself in 1547. Almost the only one in that whole movement who was not bothered by the Holy Office and forced to choose between the Reformation and the Church, Michelangelo Buonarroti also stood firm in his new understanding of faith, boldly displaying his spiritual convictions in all his remaining works of art.

The figure in the *Florentine Pietà* standing behind the body of Christ is that of the secret disciple, Joseph of Arimathea, also an idealized self-portrait of the artist in old age that is intriguing. The title "Nicodemist" was used derogatively to indicate those in Italy who commonly adhered to the doctrine of justification by faith alone. The two are linked in this New Testament account:

> After this, Joseph of Arimathea, being a disciple of Jesus, but secretly, for fear of the Jews, asked Pilate that he might take away the body of Jesus; and Pilate gave him permission. So he came and took the body of Jesus. And Nicodemus, who at first came to Jesus by night, also came, bringing a mixture of myrrh and aloes, about a hundred pounds. Then they took the body of Jesus.[13]

One story says that the sculptor was hurrying to finish the work because Urbino, a beloved assistant, was dying. There may have been a flaw in the marble, but something caused the sculptor to mutilate and abandon this pietà. Fragments of the left arm of Christ were pieced together by a student, Tiberio Calcagni, who also restored the right hand and left breast and finished (some think ruined) the Magdalene. A portion of Christ's left leg is missing; it is truly a broken body.

How fitting, I think, in this season of my own brokenness, brought about, some would say, by my own inadequate abilities. Of course, all of us are broken and unfinished. Of course, none of us, even the masters, possess expressiveness enough to convey the meanings of this broken world, or of the deepest yearnings of our souls. Words are only symbols; our thoughts are impartial. Even the most brilliant are unable to finish the work they have set out to do. I discover that tears are streaming down my cheeks.

I am so grateful for this wintry day in Italy and this early morning. No other tourists are shuffling through, no art students posturing themselves as aficionados. I have a seat from which to contemplate. It is unusually quiet. Bells ring from the Duomo Cathedral across the street. Silenced, I have nothing I must do, no place I must be. Unself-consciously, I wipe away my tears. Surely I am not the first to weep, touched by the beauties of this city. We are all in need of pity, of mercy, of compassion, of lament. In the long run, no artistry, no matter how brilliant, is enormous enough to convey the realities of pietà. The masters, as well as those of us with small gifts, know this truth. In one way or another, humility inevitably forces us to lift our hands, open. At some point, in every work, the artist finally acquiesces.

Scholars often refer to the sculptures and drawings of this final period of Michelangelo's life as *orations* or inward prayers. In fact, one of the very final works finished just before his death was another pietà now in Milan, the *Rondanini,* which some art experts have called a prayer in stone.

And that is what all this collecting has brought me to. This is what it signifies. I want to hold the broken body. I want the works of my mind and hands, the labor of my life, to be orations. I want to be a pietà.

NOTES

Chapter 1

1. Harrison Rainie, "The Buried Sounds of Children Crying," *U.S. News & World Report*, 19 April 1995, p. 10.
2. Ibid.
3. Ibid.
4. William Shakespeare, *King John*, ed. Stanley T. Williams (New Haven, Conn.: Yale University Press, 1963), p. 53.
5. *Oklahoman & Times*, 22 April 1995, quoted in Tides Foundation's *Requiem for the Heartland* (San Francisco: Collins Publishers, 1995), p. 45.
6. Dr. Billy Graham, "A Time of Healing" Prayer Service, quoted in *Requiem for the Heartland*, p. 7.
7. *Requiem for the Heartland*.
8. Peter Shaffer, *Amadeus* (New York: Harper & Row, 1981), p. 6.
9. James 2:13.
10. Psalm 86:15–16.
11. Gerard Manley Hopkins in *The Oxford Authors*, ed. Catherine Phillips (Oxford: Oxford University Press, 1986), p. 159.
12. Luke 6:36.

Chapter 2

1. William Butler Yeats, "Poem" in *The Top 500 Poems*, ed. William Harmon (New York: Columbia University Press, 1992), p. 853.
2. Matthew 26:36–38.
3. *Life*, "Historic Journey of the *Pietà*," 17 April 1964.
4. Dimitri Tselos, *The Pietà: Its Byzantine iconographic origins and its western titular diversity* (Athens, Greece: Hellenik Hetaireia Aisthetikes, 1987), p. 63. Refers to the sermon of Symeon Metaphrastes, the most reknowned of the Byzantine hagiographers (950–1000) and a historian and statesman.
5. Ibid., p. 71.
6. Ibid., p. 70. Refers to the first edition of Georgio Vasari, *The Lives of the Artists*, 1550.
7. Ibid., p. 68.
8. Matthew 26:39–40.

9. Lamentations 3:52–57.
10. George Mueller, reprint of "An Hour with George Mueller: The Man to Whom God Gave Millions" in *George Mueller Man of Faith* (Grand Rapids: Zondervan), p. 52.
11. Amy Carmichael, *Rose from Brier* (Canby, Oreg.: Christian Literature International, 1933), p. 80.

Chapter 3

1. 1 Kings 1:1–4.
2. Oliver Sacks, *An Anthropologist on Mars* (New York: Alfred A. Knopf, 1995), p. 259.
3. Ibid., p. 286.
4. Ibid., p 255.
5. Ibid., p. 265.
6. *The Illustrated Bible Dictionary*, Part 2 (Wheaton: Tynale House, 1980), p. 982.
7. Psalm 103:1–5.
8. Barbara Geub, Preface to *A Theatrical History* (New York: Vintage Books, 1974).
9. Eugene O'Neill, *A Moon for the Misbegotten*, in Geub, *A Theatrical History*, p. 92.
10. Ibid., p. 115.
11. Blaise Pascal, *Pensées*, quoted in John Bartlett, *Bartlett's Familiar Quotations* (Boston: Little, Brown & Co., 1992), p. 270.
12. Neal Postman, *Amusing Ourselves to Death: Public Discourse in the Age of Show Business* (New York: Penguin Books, 1985), p. 28.
13. Romans 12:1.
14. Exodus 25:10–22.
15. *Harper Study Bible*, ed. Harold Lindsell (Grand Rapids: Zondervan, 1952), p. 119.
16. Matthew 5:7.
17. William Shakespeare, *Coriolanus*, *The Annotated Shakespeare,* ed. Al Rouse (New York: Clarkson N. Potter, Inc., 1978), p. 64.
18. Matthew 12:7.
19. Edward W. Desmond, "Friends Who Attended," *Time*, 4 December 1989, pp. 11–34.
20. William Shakespeare, *The Merchant of Venice* 4.1, in *Shakespeare: Twenty-Three Plays and the Sonnets*, ed. Thomas Marc Parrott (New York: Charles Scribner's & Sons, 1953), pp. 237–38.

21. Ibid.
22. *Mother Teresa,* narrated by Richard Attenborough, distributed by Ignatius Press, 1986.

Chapter 4

1. Michael Kilian, "History Lesson," *Chicago Tribune*, 4 June 1995, sec. 5, p. 4.
2. *The Dictionary of National Biography*, ed. Leslie Stephen and Sidney Lee, vol. xx, since 1917, p. 571.
3. Aung San Suu Kyi, *Freedom from Fear and Other Writings*, ed. Michael Aris (New York: Viking, 1991), p. 180.
4. Randall Wallace, *Braveheart* (New York: Pocket Books, 1995), pp. 270–71.
5. Matthew 27:50–53.
6. Mark 15:37–39.
7. Luke 23:46–47.
8. Søren Kierkegaard, in *The Journal of Kierkegaard*, ed. Alexander Dru (New York: Harper & Brothers, 1995), p. 245.
9. Richard Foster, *Prayer: Finding the Heart's True Home* (San Francisco: Harper, 1992), p. 54.
10. Galatians 2:20.
11. Thomas Merton, *Seeds of Contemplation* (Norfolk, Conn.: New Directions Books, 1949), p. 24.

Chapter 5

1. Anne Lamott, *Bird by Bird* (New York: Doubleday, 1984), p. 205.
2. Anne Lamott, *Operating Instructions: A Journal of My Son's First Year* (New York & San Francisco: Pantheon Books, 1993), p. 220.
3. Ibid., pp. 30–31.
4. Mark Backlin, "Vitamin T: An Extra Dimension of Health," *Prevention* magazine, February 1996, pp. 17–18.
5. Ibid.
6. Ibid.
7. Ibid.
8. Ibid.
9. Don Allender and Tremper Longman III, *Bold Love* (Colorado Springs: NavPress, 1992), p. 212.
10. James 1:5.

Chapter 6

1. E-mail from "Jeanie" to the author, used by permission.
2. Victor Hugo, *Les Miserables* (London: George Routledge & Sons, Ltd., n.d.), p. 397.
3. Colossians 1:9–11.
4. Hugo, *Les Miserables*, p. 411.
5. Romans 12:6, 8.
6. Tom Howard, *The Novels of Charles Williams* (San Francisco: Ignatius Press, 1983), pp. 25–26.
7. 2 Corinthians 1:3–7.
8. Peter M. Senge, *The Fifth Discipline* (New York: Currency Doubleday, 1990), p. 7.
9. David and Karen Mains, *Tales of the Restoration* (Colorado Springs: Chariot Books, 1996), p. 49.
10. Doris Lessing, *The Diary of a Good Neighbor* (New York: Alfred A. Knopf, 1983), p. 237.
11. Lessing, *Diary*, p. 232.
12. Matthew 15:22.
13. Wilma Burton, *I Need a Miracle Today, Lord* (Chicago: Moody Press, 1976), p. 23.
14. Matthew 20:30.
15. Matthew 20:34.

Chapter 7

1. Esther de Wall, *Seeking God* (Collegeville, Minn.: The Liturgical Press, 1984), p. 70.
2. Ibid., p. 72.
3. Romans 6:2–4, 13.
4. Alice Mary Hadfield, *Charles Williams: An Exploration of His Life and Work* (New York: Oxford University Press, 1983), p. 215.
5. 2 Corinthians 1:3–4.
6. Philip Brooks, as recorded in my personal journal. For some years, I have collected spiritual and literary quotations that seemed to speak directly to me and to my experience of life. I recorded these in my personal journal but, unfortunately, was not thinking of publishing during these times of prayerful meditation.
7. George A. Panichas, *The Burden of Vision: Dostoyevsky's Spiritual Art* (Chicago: Gateway Editions, 1985), p. 9.

8. Feodor Mikhailovich Dostoyevsky, *The Idiot* (New York: Modern Library, 1983), p. 578.
9. Ibid., p. 580.
10. Ibid., p. 583.
11. Ibid.

Chapter 8

1. Hamalian and Volpe, Leo Tolstoy's "The Death of Ivan Ilych" in *Ten Modern Short Novels* (New York: G. P. Putnam & Sons, 1958), p. 37.
2. Ibid., p. 37.
3. Ibid., p. 38.
4. Ibid.
5. Robert Munsch, *Love You Forever* (Willowdale, Ontario: Firefly Books, Ltd., 1994).
6. Ibid.
7. A. W. Tozer, as recorded in my personal journal.
8. 1 John 1:8; 2:9.
9. Hamalian and Volpe, *Short Novels*, p. 38.
10. Ibid., p. 40.
11. Ibid., p. 39.
12. Ibid.
13. Genesis 3:9.
14. Genesis 3:13.
15. Genesis 4:6.
16. Genesis 18:9.
17. 1 Kings 19:9.
18. Isaiah 6:8.
19. Luke 5:23.
20. Luke 5:34.
21. Luke 6:9.
22. Luke 8:25.
23. Mark 5:9.
24. Mark 5:30.
25. Matthew 16:13, 15; Mark 8:27, 29.
26. Luke 10:26.
27. John 21:15.
28. James 1:22.
29. Amy Carmichael, *If* (Grand Rapids: Zondervan Publishing, 1967).

30. Corrie ten Boom, as recorded in my personal journal.
31. Hamalian and Volpe, *Short Novels*, p. 47.
32. Ibid., p. 51.
33. Ibid., p. 54.
34. Oswald Chambers, as recorded in my personal journal.
35. Hamalian and Volpe, *Short Novels*, p. 10.

Chapter 9

1. 2 Chronicles 20:3.
2. 2 Chronicles 20:15, 17.
3. Eugene Peterson, *The Message* (Colorado Springs: NavPress, 1993), p. 47.
4. Copied from a Sunday worship bulletin. No source given.
5. John Irving, *A Prayer for Owen Meany* (New York: Ballantine Books, 1989), p. 614.
6. Ibid., p. 1.
7. R. Z. Sheppard, *Time*, 3 April 1989, p. 80.
8. James M. Wall, "Owen Meany and the Presence of God," 22–29 March 1989, p. 299.
9. Irving, *Owen Meany*, p. 447.
10. Ibid., p. 10.
11. Ibid., p. 341.
12. Ibid., p. 1.
13. Tozer, as recorded in my personal journal.

Chapter 10

1. Sister Helen Prejean, *Dead Man Walking* (New York: Vintage Books, 1994), p. 1.
2. Ibid., p. 47.
3. Ibid., p. 49.
4. Lois Forer, *Money and Justice* (New York: Norton, 1984), p. 9, quoted in Prejean, *Dead Man*, p. 252.
5. Emily Dickinson, no. 341, *The Complete Poems of Emily Dickinson*, ed. Thomas H. Johnson (Boston: Little, Brown & Co., 1960), p. 162.
6. Alex Lasker and Bill Rubenstein, *Beyond Rangoon* (Los Angeles: Castlerock Entertainment, 1996), John Boorman film.
7. 1 Peter 4:12–19.
8. Carmichael, *Rose from Brier*, p. 92.

9. Daniel Goleman, Ph.D., *Emotional Intelligence: Why It Can Matter More Than IQ* (New York: Bantam Books, 1995), p. 43.
10. Ibid., p. 47.
11. F. Frangipane, "Accuser of the Brethren" (Cedar Rapids: Advancing Church Ministries, 1991), p. 9.
12. Ibid., p. 9, 1.
13. E. Herman, *Creative Prayer* (Cincinnati: Forward Movement Publication, n.d.), p. 34.
14. Philippians 2:5–8.
15. Robertson of Brighton, quoted in Herman, *Creative Prayer*, p. 98.
16. As recorded in my personal journal.
17. Prejean, *Dead Man*, p. 81.
18. 1 Timothy 1:15.
19. Prejean, *Dead Man*, p. 20.
20. Marietta Jaeger on *Oprah*, 18 January 1996.
21. Ibid.
22. Letter reprinted by consent of the writer.

Chapter 11

1. Edna St. Vincent Millay, "Conscientious Objector," quoted by Maya Angelou on *Sunday Morning*, 17 January 1993.
2. 2 Corinthians 5:18–19.
3. Isaiah 59:9–10.
4. Merton, *Seeds of Contemplation*, p. 184.
5. Ibid., p. 39.
6. Hebrews 10:10–12.
7. Matthew 25:41–46.
8. Matthew 25:31–32.
9. Romans 4:16–18.

Chapter 12

1. 2 Corinthians 4:7–11.
2. Lamott, *Operating Instructions*, p. 27.
3. Ibid., pp. 27–28.
4. *Bridge of Hope Newsletter*, Bridge of Hope Publications, Fall 1993.
5. *Mentor's Resource Guide: A guide to mentoring homeless families* (Coatesville, Penn.: Bridge of Hope Publications).
6. Ibid. Refers to an article in the *Philadelphia Inquirer*, 9 May 1992.

Chapter 13

1. Joseph Bernardin, as reported in Commemorative section, *Chicago Tribune*, p. 7.
2. Edward F. Hoover, "We came to believe in him," *Chicago Tribune*, 17 November 1996, sec. 1, p. 21.
3. Joseph Bernardin, as reported in Commemorative section, *Chicago Tribune*, 17 November 1996, sec. 2, p. 6.
4. Ibid.
5. Ibid., p. 3.
6. Ibid., p. 8.
7. John Kass, "Cemetery route reaches out to all," *Chicago Tribune*, 19 November 1996, pp. 1, 18.

Chapter 14

1. Proverbs 10:12.
2. Job 23:10, 12.
3. Steve Camp and Rob Frazier, "Mercy in the Wilderness" (Warner Brothers Records, Inc., 1994).

Afterword

1. Georgio Vasari, *The Lives of the Artists* (Oxford: Oxford University Press), p. 479.
2. Charles de Tolnay, *Michelangelo* (Princeton: Princeton University Press, 1975), p. 108.
3. Ibid., p. 103.
4. Romans 3:28.
5. John C. Zimmermn, *A Christian Analysis of the Life of Michelangelo as a Model for Clarifying the Nature of Christian Cultural Criticism* (San Anselmo, Calif.: San Francisco Theological Seminary, 1977), p. 183.
6. Tolney, p. 104.
7. Ibid., p. 101.
8. Ibid., p. 106.
9. Ibid., p. 106.
10. Zimmerman, p. 232.
11. Zimmerman, p. 205.
12. Ibid., p. 208.
13. John 19:38–40.

ABOUT THE AUTHOR

Karen Mains is an award-winning author and communicator and is actively involved in radio and television broadcasting. She served on the board of InterVarsity Christian Fellowship for eight years and was elected the first woman chairperson. She is now a member of the executive team of The Chapel Ministries, which produces a daily, half-hour national television show, "You Need to Know."

ABOUT "A MODERN PIETÀ"

The painting by Mary Porterfield in chapter 10 is on display at St. Louis University Hospital. Porterfield, a former student aide at the hospital, says the violence she saw there inspired the painting. Copies of the artwork can be purchased for $13.50 (includes shipping and handling). Send your money to:

Sandy Spencer, Pastoral Care
St. Louis University Hospital
Vista at Grand Boulevard
St. Louis, MO 63110

All proceeds from the sales go to support the St. Louis University Hospital Response to Community Violence, a violence prevention program.